SURVI MURDER
WHEN FATE LEAVES YOU BEHIND

WRITTEN BY
STUART ABREY

EDITED AND DESIGNED BY
STUART ABREY

COVER PHOTOGRAPHY BY
BOKHABINYANA JOSEPHINE ABREY

COVER IMAGE: THE AUTHOR
LOOKING ACROSS THE OCEAN,
FROM EUROPE (PORTUGAL) TO AFRICA (MOROCCO).

SURVIVING MURDER

WHEN FATE LEAVES YOU BEHIND

LOVELIGHT
Publications ©

ISBN: 978 – 1 – 9997018 – 5 – 7

COPYRIGHT© STUART ABREY 2023

THIS BOOK IS WRITTEN IN LARGE CAPITALS
FOR EASIER READING

All rights reserved

THIS BOOK IS

FOR MY DAUGHTER, KaRa;

FOR THE SAKE OF ALL OUR CHILDREN;

FOR VICTIMS AND THEIR FAMILIES;

FOR THE PERPETRATORS;

FOR CHANGE;

FOR A
BETTER
WORLD;

FOR
HOPE;

FOR
LOVE;

FOR
YOU;

FOR GOOD,
FOREVERMORE!

FOR
MY WIFE.
BOKHABINYANA.
A SHINING STAR
I WISH ON
EVERY
DAY.

A SHOOTING STAR
THAT TWINKLED IN AND OUT
OF MY WORLD
FAR TOO QUICKLY.

A STAR THAT DAZZLED US ALL
WITH HER BRILLIANCE.

A STAR WHOSE LIGHT
SHALL BRIGHTEN MY FACE
AGAIN SOME DAY...

...WITH KaRa, OUR STAR OF LIFE,
"NALEDI YA BOPHELO"

THIS BOOK IS

FOR MY DAUGHTER, KaRa;

FOR THE SAKE OF ALL OUR CHILDREN;

FOR VICTIMS AND THEIR FAMILIES;

FOR THE PERPETRATORS;

FOR CHANGE;

FOR A
BETTER
WORLD;

FOR
HOPE;

FOR
LOVE;

FOR
YOU;

FOR GOOD,
FOREVERMORE!

**FOR
MY WIFE.
BOKHABINYANA.
A SHINING STAR
I WISH ON
EVERY
DAY.**

**A SHOOTING STAR
THAT TWINKLED IN AND OUT
OF MY WORLD
FAR TOO QUICKLY.**

**A STAR THAT DAZZLED US ALL
WITH HER BRILLIANCE.**

**A STAR WHOSE LIGHT
SHALL BRIGHTEN MY FACE
AGAIN SOME DAY...**

**...WITH KaRa, OUR STAR OF LIFE,
"NALEDI YA BOPHELO"**

CONTENTS

Preface P. i

INTRODUCTION P. 1

CH. 1 IN THE BEGINNING P. 3

CH. 2 HAPPINESS P. 9

CH. 3 BACK TO AFRICA P. 20

"KaRa BOPHELO ASHENAFI ABREY"
– A POEM BY KHABI P. 30

CH. 4 DEATH AT THE DOOR P. 34

CH. 5 THE AFTERMATH P. 45

CH. 6 THE THINGS PEOPLE SAY! P. 55

CH. 7 DAGGER TO THE HEART P. 61

CH. 8 THE FUNERAL P. 72

CH. 9 THE TRIAL, BY FIRE P. 90

CH. 10 MIRACLES MEANWHILE P. 117

CH. 11 THE BABY COMMUNICATES! P. 143

CH. 12 CONCLUSIONS P. 150

CH. 13 A MESSAGE TO THE BEREAVED P. 156

CH. 14 MESSAGE TO A KILLER P. 170

CH. 15 HEALING P. 181

CH. 16 SURVIVAL GUIDE P. 191

AFTERWORD P. 223

NOTES P. 228

Preface

DEAR READER,
I WRITE THIS BOOK,
BECAUSE SOMEBODY'S GOTTA DO SOMETHING...
...ANYTHING...
...IN AN ATTEMPT TO REDUCE THE PAIN
FELT IN THIS WORLD.

I ENDEAVOUR TO COMFORT AND COACH
THOSE WHO HAVE LOST LOVED ONES
IN TRAGIC, SHOCKING CIRCUMSTANCES,
USING MY EXPERIENCES AS A GUIDE.

I ALSO WANT THOSE WHO FEEL NO WAY
TO TAKE ANOTHERS LIFE, OR THEIR OWN,
TO UNDERSTAND THE GRAVITY
OF THEIR ACTIONS,
EXPLAINING QUITE CLEARLY,
HOW DEVASTATING AND FAR REACHING
THE ACT OF TAKING A LIFE IS.

TELL ME SOMETHING...
ARE YOU HAPPY WITH THE WORLD?
NEITHER AM I! SO INSTEAD OF MAKING IT WORSE,
LET'S ENSURE THE WORLD HAS GOOD THINGS IN IT
BY PUTTING THEM THERE.

INSTEAD OF FIGHTING AGAINST EACH OTHER,
LET'S FIGHT AGAINST THE SUFFERING.

**LOVE NEEDS TO RECLAIM HER PLACE
IN THE FOREFRONT OF OUR HEARTS AND MINDS.**

WE REVOLT, NOT WITH ARMS AND MORE SUFFERING,
BUT BY LIVING OUR LIVES POSITIVELY,
IN THE KNOWLEDGE AND COMFORT
OF THE ETERNAL TRUTHS;
NOT WITH FORCE, BUT BY
BEHAVING AS AN EXAMPLE
OF HOW PEOPLE SHOULD BE;
BY TREATING OTHERS
AS YOURSELF,
AS IF WE WERE ALL ONE,
BECAUSE, IN TRUTH,
**WE REALLY ARE
ALL ONE.**

EVERYTHING WE DO THAT IS GOOD,
IS OF A CERTAIN VIBRATION
THAT IS UNSTOPPABLE.
IT WILL RIPPLE THROUGHOUT THE UNIVERSE!

IT IS SOUL-NOURISHMENT,
ON A PERSONAL LEVEL
AND ON A GLOBAL SCALE,
BECAUSE WE ARE ALL ONE.
IT IS UPLIFTING FOR ALL.

HOWEVER, THAT WHICH WE DO THAT IS BAD,
JUST BRINGS EVERYONE AND OURSELVES DOWN.
WHAT'S THE USE IN THAT?

Preface

DEAR READER,
I WRITE THIS BOOK,
BECAUSE SOMEBODY'S GOTTA DO SOMETHING...
...*ANYTHING*...
...IN AN ATTEMPT TO REDUCE THE PAIN
FELT IN THIS WORLD.

I ENDEAVOUR TO COMFORT AND COACH
THOSE WHO HAVE LOST LOVED ONES
IN TRAGIC, SHOCKING CIRCUMSTANCES,
USING MY EXPERIENCES AS A GUIDE.

I ALSO WANT THOSE WHO FEEL NO WAY
TO TAKE ANOTHERS LIFE, OR THEIR OWN,
TO UNDERSTAND THE GRAVITY
OF THEIR ACTIONS,
EXPLAINING QUITE CLEARLY,
HOW DEVASTATING AND FAR REACHING
THE ACT OF TAKING A LIFE IS.

TELL ME SOMETHING...
ARE YOU HAPPY WITH THE WORLD?
NEITHER AM I! SO INSTEAD OF MAKING IT WORSE,
LET'S ENSURE THE WORLD HAS GOOD THINGS IN IT
BY PUTTING THEM THERE.

INSTEAD OF FIGHTING AGAINST EACH OTHER,
LET'S FIGHT AGAINST THE SUFFERING.

**LOVE NEEDS TO RECLAIM HER PLACE
IN THE FOREFRONT OF OUR HEARTS AND MINDS.**

WE REVOLT, NOT WITH ARMS AND MORE SUFFERING,
BUT BY LIVING OUR LIVES POSITIVELY,
IN THE KNOWLEDGE AND COMFORT
OF THE ETERNAL TRUTHS;
NOT WITH FORCE, BUT BY
BEHAVING AS AN EXAMPLE
OF HOW PEOPLE SHOULD BE;
BY TREATING OTHERS
AS YOURSELF,
AS IF WE WERE ALL ONE,
BECAUSE, IN TRUTH,
**WE REALLY ARE
ALL ONE.**

EVERYTHING WE DO THAT IS GOOD,
IS OF A CERTAIN VIBRATION
THAT IS UNSTOPPABLE.
IT WILL RIPPLE THROUGHOUT THE UNIVERSE!

IT IS SOUL-NOURISHMENT,
ON A PERSONAL LEVEL
AND ON A GLOBAL SCALE,
BECAUSE WE ARE ALL ONE.
IT IS UPLIFTING FOR ALL.

HOWEVER, THAT WHICH WE DO THAT IS BAD,
JUST BRINGS EVERYONE AND OURSELVES DOWN.
WHAT'S THE USE IN THAT?

**LET US STRIVE TO BRING JOY, NOT PAIN,
INTO OUR LIVES AND THE LIVES OF OTHERS.**

WE MUST REALIZE THAT, DUE TO OUR ONE-NESS,
THE NEGATIVITY WE POUR OUT ONTO OTHERS
WE ACTUALLY POUR ON OUR OWN HEADS.

WOULDN'T YOU RATHER BLESSINGS
CAME POURING DOWN ON YOU!?!

THEN **BE GOOD.**

THE EMOTIONS AND FEELINGS
WE CAUSE OTHERS TO FEEL,
SHALL SOMEDAY BE
OUR UN-ENDING REALITY!

**SO, BE GOOD TO YOURSELF,
*BY BEING GOOD TO OTHERS!***

AS FOR THOSE WHO ARE
SURVIVING THE MURDER OF A LOVED ONE,
I WANT TO BE HERE FOR YOU
IN THE SENSE THAT
YOU WILL NOT FEEL SO ALONE
AND I WANT TO SHARE WITH YOU
THE THINGS THAT HAVE GOT ME THROUGH
THE WORST NIGHTMARE OF MY LIFE.

I WANT YOU TO KNOW
THAT ALL IS NOT AS IT SEEMS.

JUSTICE *WILL* PREVAIL IN THE END,
EVEN IF IT DOESN'T SEEM TO!

I WILL PROVE TO YOU THAT THERE *IS* HOPE,
BECAUSE THERE IS MORE TO LIFE
THAN ALL THAT MEETS THE EYE.

I WANT TO HELP YOU RECOVER
AND GET YOURSELF FUNCTIONING
AT A POSITIVE LEVEL AGAIN.

PEOPLE ARE PROBABLY WORRIED ABOUT YOU.
YOU MAY BE DRINKING HEAVILY
OR TAKING DRUGS.
YOU MAY BE LOSING THE DESIRE
TO BOTHER TO LOOK AFTER YOURSELF
OR EVEN KEEP GOING.

BUT WAIT!
**YOU'RE STILL LOVED
BY THE ONE YOU'VE LOST!**

DO YOUR BEST FOR THEM,
BY DOING THE BEST FOR YOURSELF.

LOVE YOURSELF AGAIN.
LOVE LIFE AGAIN!
ALL IS NOT LOST!
THERE IS HOPE!

TO VICTIMS' FAMILIES AND TO PERPETRATORS...

...IT'S NOT TOO LATE!

IT'S NOT TOO LATE
TO SPEAK TO THE ONES WE HAVE LOST;

TO GET ANSWERS;

TO GET JUSTICE;

TO FIND A NEW PERSPECTIVE;

TO HAVE A CHANGE OF MIND;

TO BE SAVED FROM PAIN;

TO FIND HAPPINESS;

TO BE FORGIVEN;

TO BE LOVED;

TO SMILE;

TO TURN IT ALL AROUND;

TO BE HEARD AND UNDERSTOOD;

TO MAKE A POSITIVE DIFFERENCE;

TO CHANGE THE WORLD FOR THE BETTER;

FOR GOOD TO BE VICTORIOUS, AGAINST ALL ODDS!

DEAR ONES MOURNING,

AS YOU SHALL SURELY SEE IN THIS BOOK,
ALL IS NOT AS IT SEEMS IN THIS WORLD.
THERE IS NO NEED FOR YOU TO HURT
QUITE SO SORELY.

DRY YOUR TEARS SISTER/BROTHER,
READ CAREFULLY WHAT THIS BOOK SAYS AND
HOPEFULLY, NAY, SURELY, THE TRUTH HEREIN,
SHALL SET YOUR HEART AND MIND FREE
FROM SEEMINGLY INESCAPABLE SORROW.

DEAR ONES ACTING GRIEVOUSLEY,

AS YOU SHALL SEE IN THIS BOOK,
IT IS OF UTMOST IMPORTANCE
THAT YOU CHANGE YOUR REALITY,
NOT JUST FOR YOUR VICTIMS SAKE...
...BUT FOR YOUR OWN.

YOU SEE, JUSTICE IS INESCAPABLE,
HOWEVER, FORGIVENESS AND MERCY
ARE ALWAYS AVAILABLE.

WHAT YOU DO NOW,
IS OF VITAL IMPORTANCE TO YOU.
PLEASE TRY TO BE GOOD!

YOURS TRULY, FAITHFULLY AND ETERNALLY,
      YOUR BROTHER, STUART.

28th JUNE, 2023

...IT'S NOT TOO LATE!
IT'S NOT TOO LATE
TO SPEAK TO THE ONES WE HAVE LOST;

TO GET ANSWERS;

TO GET JUSTICE;

TO FIND A NEW PERSPECTIVE;

TO HAVE A CHANGE OF MIND;

TO BE SAVED FROM PAIN;

TO FIND HAPPINESS;

TO BE FORGIVEN;

TO BE LOVED;

TO SMILE;

TO TURN IT ALL AROUND;

TO BE HEARD AND UNDERSTOOD;

TO MAKE A POSITIVE DIFFERENCE;

TO CHANGE THE WORLD FOR THE BETTER;

FOR GOOD TO BE VICTORIOUS, AGAINST ALL ODDS!

DEAR ONES MOURNING,

AS YOU SHALL SURELY SEE IN THIS BOOK,
ALL IS NOT AS IT SEEMS IN THIS WORLD.
THERE IS NO NEED FOR YOU TO HURT
QUITE SO SORELY.

DRY YOUR TEARS SISTER/BROTHER,
READ CAREFULLY WHAT THIS BOOK SAYS AND
HOPEFULLY, NAY, SURELY, THE TRUTH HEREIN,
SHALL SET YOUR HEART AND MIND FREE
FROM SEEMINGLY INESCAPABLE SORROW.

DEAR ONES ACTING GRIEVOUSLEY,

AS YOU SHALL SEE IN THIS BOOK,
IT IS OF UTMOST IMPORTANCE
THAT YOU CHANGE YOUR REALITY,
NOT JUST FOR YOUR VICTIMS SAKE…
…BUT FOR YOUR OWN.

YOU SEE, JUSTICE IS INESCAPABLE,
HOWEVER, FORGIVENESS AND MERCY
ARE ALWAYS AVAILABLE.

WHAT YOU DO NOW,
IS OF VITAL IMPORTANCE TO YOU.
PLEASE TRY TO BE GOOD!

YOURS TRULY, FAITHFULLY AND ETERNALLY,
      YOUR BROTHER, STUART.

28th JUNE, 2023

THIS BOOK BY NO MEANS
COVERS ALL THE ASPECTS OF EMOTIONS
AND REACTIONS TO THE EVENTS DETAILED HERE.

IT IS SIMPLY AN OUTLINE
OF MY EXPERIENCE,
AVOIDING OVER ELABORATION
TO MAKE THE BOOK MORE ACCESSIBLE.

WHEN GETTING FEEDBACK FROM FRIENDS,
REGARDING MY FIRST BOOK,
IT CAME TO LIGHT THAT SOME PEOPLE,
MYSELF INCLUDED, BEING A SLOW READER,
FIND THICK BOOKS TOO DAUNTING TO START,
OR TOO LONG TO HAVE TIME TO READ IT.

ALSO, I FIND THAT A MASS OF WORDS
PUTS ME OFF READING SOME ARTICLES,
PREFERRING TO READ
SMALL BLOCKS OF WRITING WITH PICTURES.

THIS IS WHY THE FORMAT
OF THE BOOK IS THE WAY IT IS,
BECAUSE I WANT EVERYBODY
WHO NEEDS TO KNOW AND UNDERSTAND
THE FULLNESS OF THIS BOOK
TO BE ABLE TO DO SO.

I DON'T WRITE FOR THE SAKE OF IT.
NOR DO MANY READERS, FOR VARIOUS REASONS,
HAVE THE ABILITY TO SIT AND READ
SOME WEIGHTY TOME.

I JUST WANT TO GET THE MESSAGE ACROSS
AS SIMPLY AND AS QUICKLY AS POSSIBLE,
SO AS TO EFFECT A POSITIVE CHANGE
IN THE READER AS SOON AS POSSIBLE.

I DONT WANT TO RAMBLE.
I WANT EACH PAGE TO COUNT.
EVEN IF YOU JUST READ ONE RANDOM PAGE,
I WANT THAT ONE PAGE TO MOVE YOU;
TO MAKE A LASTING IMPRESSION ON YOU.

I WANT IT TO CHANGE YOU SOMEHOW,
WHETHER IT BE YOU FEEL LIGHTER,
FEEL LIFTED, COMFORTED, VALIDATED,
UNDERSTOOD, SUPPORTED, ENLIGHTENED,
HEALED OR HOPEFUL.

MAYBE YOU FEEL REMORSE,
IF YOU HAVE CAUSED PAIN.
MAYBE YOU WANT TO DO GOOD
FROM THIS MOMENT FORTH.
MAYBE YOU WANT TO GIVE YOURSELF
A CHANCE OF HAPPINESS
BY TURNING YOUR BACK ON YOUR NEGATIVE PAST.
MAYBE, YOU TOO, FEEL HEALED AND HOPEFUL.

I HOPE SO. I HOPE ALL WHO READ THIS
BENEFIT IN SOME WAY,
CONTRIBUTING TO A BETTER EXPERIENCE
FOR US ALL!
ONE ETERNAL LOVE!

INTRODUCTION

GREETINGS, IN THE NAME OF LOVE AND TRUTH.
I WOULD LIKE TO SHARE SOMETHING
WITH YOU....OR RATHER,
I FEEL I *NEED* TO SHARE SOMETHING
WITH YOU AND THE WORLD,
IN AN ATTEMPT TO CHANGE IT
AS BEST WE CAN.

IT'S GOOD NEWS AND BAD NEWS I'M AFRAID
AND I DON'T RELISH SHARING IT WITH ANYONE.
HOWEVER, **I HOPE** THAT TELLING
AS MANY PEOPLE AS POSSIBLE
WHAT I'VE BEEN EXPERIENCING, WILL;

a) **LEAD TO INNER PEACE FOR THOSE
WHO'VE HAD LOVED ONES TAKEN FROM THEM,**

b) **MAKE PEOPLE THINK TWICE**
ABOUT THEIR ACTIONS,
BEFORE INFLICTING GRIEVOUS HARM,
UPON OTHERS....**OR** THEMSELVES,
LEADING, *HOPEFULLY,* TO,

c) A **CHANGE** IN **PEOPLE'S MINDEST**
AND BEHAVIOUR, **LEADING TO MORE PEACE,**
SECURITY **AND HAPPINESS IN THE WORLD.**

SOMEBODY'S GOTTA DO SOMETHING.
THINGS CAN'T STAY THE WAY THEY ARE.

I'M GOING TO TELL YOU ABOUT AN AWFUL EVENT THAT *WAS PREVENTABLE*...
...AND THE SAD TRUTH IS
THAT AFTER "JUSTICE BEING SERVED"
AND "LESSONS BEING LEARNED",
SOMETHING LIKE WHAT HAPPENED...
...WILL PROBABLY HAPPEN AGAIN.
AND AGAIN...AND AGAIN...AND AGAIN,
BECAUSE, ACCORDING TO THE STATISTICS,
"SIMILAR" EVENTS TAKE PLACE *TWICE A WEEK!*

THIS IS WHY IT FEELS ESPECIALLY URGENT
TO MAKE AS MANY PEOPLE AS POSSIBLE
HEAR ABOUT WHAT HAS HAPPENED
**IN THE HOPE OF SOMEONE
WITH THE POWER TO END
THIS REPEATING PATTERN OF PAIN,**
DOES SO AS A RESULT OF DISCOVERING
WHAT HAS HAPPENED TO MY BEAUTIFUL FAMILY.

THE PAIN I FEEL...NO ONE SHOULD EVER FEEL...
YET MILLIONS MORE AROUND THE WORLD
ARE FEELING SIMILAR PAIN TO MINE,
BECAUSE OF WAR AND VIOLENCE
AND LACK OF CARE IN MENTAL HEALTH,
**BECAUSE THERE ISN'T ENOUGH
CARE IN THE SYSTEM, OR
LOVE IN THE LAW.
THE WORLD *MUST* CHANGE!**

SO, TO THAT END/BEGINNING,
HERE IS OUR BEAUTIFUL, TRAGIC STORY...

CHAPTER 1...IN THE BEGINNING

GOING RIGHT BACK TO THE START;
I WAS BORN IN ESSEX ON THE
30TH OF JULY, 1978,
IN THE HEIGHT OF THE ENGLISH SUMMER.
MY WIFE, KHABI, WAS BORN IN SOWETO ON THE
30TH OF DECEMBER, 1985,
IN THE HEIGHT OF THE SOUTH AFRICAN SUMMER.

HER FULL NAME, BOKHABINYANA, MEANS
"RADIANCE", IN HER MOTHER TONGUE, SETSWANA.

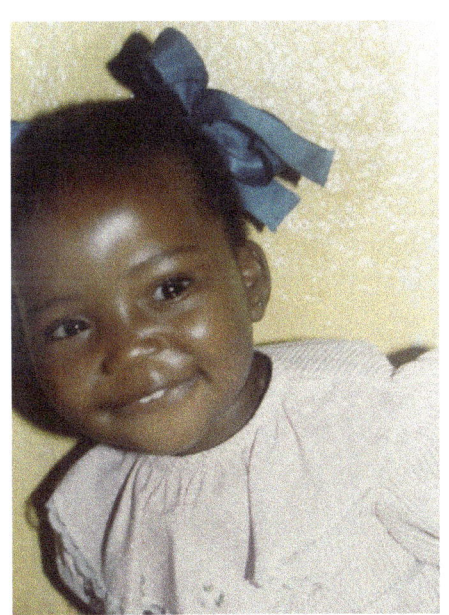

WHAT A PERFECT NAME
FOR A SOUL THAT SO SHINETH!
PURE SUNSHINE!

MEETING EACH OTHER WAS THE REWARD
FOR MANY A TEAR SHED:

BACK IN 2007, IN WOOD GREEN, NORTH LONDON,
I WAS WORKING AS A SUPPORT WORKER
FOR ADULTS WITH LEARNING DISABILITIES.
MY GIRLFRIEND-AT-THE-TIME, MAAME,
WAS A CARER FROM TAKORADI, GHANA.

ONE DAY, I'D FORGOTTEN MY PHONE AT HOME.
NO BIGGIE TO ME, MY PHONE RARELY RINGS,
BUT WHEN I GOT HOME FROM WORK,
MAAME TOLD ME I'D HAD LOADS OF MISSED CALLS,
SO MANY THAT SHE SAID IT SCARED HER.

IMMEDIATELY I WAS TROUBLED.
I CHECKED MY PHONE.
I HAD SEVERAL MISSED CALLS FROM MY MUM
AND A WHOLE LIST OF CALLS FROM MY UNCLE,
MY DAD'S BROTHER, LARRY.
HE *NEVER* CALLS ME. MY HEART SANK.
I KNEW SOMETHING WAS WRONG WITH MY
STEP-DAD-FROM-BIRTH,
RICHARD/RICK.

I HAD NO CREDIT TO CALL ANYONE,
SO I RUSHED TO THE SHOP TO TOP-UP.
THE WHOLE WAY TO THE SHOP
I WAS THINKING,
"PLEASE LET HIM BE OK, PLEASE LET HIM BE OK!"
BUT DEEP DOWN....I KNEW THIS WAS *BAD*.

I CALLED MY MUM, SANDY, WHEN I GOT BACK IN.
"OH STU!......IT'S RICKY!", SHE STARTED.

THIS IS ME: "WHAT!?! WHA'S 'APPENED???"

"HE'S....HE DIED!"

"WHAT!!!??? HOW???"

"HE TOOK HIS LIIIIIFE!"

WE BOTH JUST CRUMBLED IN TEARS.

BORN ON 24TH OF DECEMBER, 1943,
DURING THE SECOND WORLD WAR,
"WHILE BOMBS WERE DROPPING",
MY DAD WAS MY GUARDIAN ANGEL.

MY DAD WITH "DADA" MADIBA (MR MANDELA)

HE HANGED HIMSELF ON
3RD OF JANUARY, 2007,
JUST 10 DAYS AFTER HIS 63RD BIRTHDAY.

MY NAN, HIS MUM, "DOT",
HAD DIED THE YEAR BEFORE
AND MY DAD HAD ALWAYS SAID,
"WHEN SHE GOES, I'LL BE IN AFTER HER."
NO ONE REALISED HE WAS BEING SERIOUS.

TWO WEEKS OR SO, AFTER HE DIED,
I HAD A DREAM OF HIM.
IN IT, I ASKED HIM, "WHAT HAPPENED…
…WHY DIDN'T YOU TALK TO ME!?!"

HE JUST CHANGED THE SUBJECT.
I PUT MY ARM AROUND HIS SHOULDERS
AND I COULD ACTUALLY FEEL HIS SHOULDER
AS I STRUGGLED TO REACH HIS HEIGHT.

THE DREAM WENT ON.
HE TOOK ME TO KEDDIES,
A BIG DEPARTMENT STORE IN SOUTHEND,
WHERE HE ONCE WORKED.
IT'S NOT THERE ANYMORE.

WE CARRIED ON TALKING,
THEN I FOUND MYSELF NEAR MY OLD HOME.
I WAS CRYING. I DIDN'T WANT MY DAD TO GO.
HE KNELT ON THE PAVEMENT AND HELD ME,
AS IF I WAS NOW A SMALL CHILD AGAIN.
THEN I WOKE UP…IN TEARS.

AS I CALMED MYSELF,
I NOTICED A SONG IN MY HEAD.
IT WAS LEONA LEWIS, SINGING,
"SOME PEOPLE WAIT A LIFETIME
FOR A MOMENT LIKE THIS!"

WOW!!! SO TRUE, YOU DON'T NORMALLY GET TO SEE
YOUR LOST LOVED ONES UNTIL YOU JOIN THEM...
...BUT I'D JUST HAD A MOMENT WITH MY DAD
IN THIS VISION, FOR THIS WAS NO MERE DREAM!

I WENT TO CALL MY MUM TO TELL HER,
BUT IT WAS STILL EARLY, SO I LEFT IT.
LATER....SHE CALLED ME...
..."DID YOU SEE HIM LAST NIGHT???"
WERE HER FIRST WORDS TO ME!

"YEEESSSS!!!" I SAID, ABSOLUTELY SHOCKED.
THEN SHE TOPPED IT OFF WITH,
"OH GOOD, I'M GLAD, BECAUSE
HE CAME TO SEE ME LAST NIGHT...
...AND YOU WERE WITH HIM!"

IN HER DREAM, MY DAD SLOWLY GOT YOUNGER UNTIL
HIS THICK GREY HAIR WAS FULLY BACK TO BLACK.
THE DATE WE HAD THAT DREAM WAS
19TH OF JANUARY, WHICH WAS HIS MUM'S
– AND MY MUM'S MUM'S – BIRTHDAY!
PROOF THEY WERE ALL TOGETHER AGAIN;
PROOF OF ETERNAL LIFE!
AFTER THAT I HAD MANY MORE SIGNS FROM HIM.

THAT BEING SAID, I STILL WASN'T COPING WELL.
I BLAMED MYSELF FOR BEING A CARER AND
NOT NOTICING MY DAD WAS BECOMING DEPRESSED.
I *WAS* CONCERNED ABOUT HIM...
...BUT I FELT LIKE I DIDN'T DO ENOUGH TO HELP HIM.

I KEPT BREAKING INTO TEARS
AND MY MOOD WAS GOING DOWN HILL.
IT ALL TOOK A TOLL ON MY RELATIONSHIP,
WHICH ENDED IN EMOTIONAL TURMOIL.
MAAME MOVED BACK TO GHANA,
AFTER 3 YEARS TOGETHER AND, APPARENTLY,
SHE SADLY DIED THERE, SOME YEARS LATER!

I FOUND MYSELF LIVING ALONE IN MY DAD'S FLAT,
WHICH WAS ORIGINALLY MY NAN'S FLAT.
I REMEMBER GOING THERE AS A TODDLER IN THE 70's
AND BEING TOO SMALL TO SEE OUT THE WINDOWS.

THERE WERE SOME GOOD MEMORIES THERE,
BUT NOW, ALL I COULD THINK ABOUT
WAS MY DAD DOING WHAT HE DID;
HOW DESPERATE HE MUST'VE FELT;
HOW SCARY IT MUST'VE BEEN.
TO DEFEAT THESE THOUGHTS, I SAT WHERE HE DIED
AND VISUALISED EVERYTHING I COULD
ABOUT HOW HE MUST HAVE PASSED....IT HURT,
BUT IT LEFT ME WITH NOTHING MORE TO IMAGINE.

I TRIED MY BEST TO BE POSITIVE AND
GET ON WITH LIFE, BUT STILL FELT SO PESIMISTIC, EVEN
BEGINNING TO STOP BELIEVING IN LOVE, UNTIL...

CHAPTER 2...HAPPINESS

HAVING MOVED HOME
FROM LONDON TO SOUTHEND, I BEGAN TO SEE
AN AFRICAN COUPLE AROUND TOWN,
WHO HAD SOME AMAZING DREADLOCKS!
BEING A RASTAMAN WITH DREADLOCKS TOO,
I GOT REASONING WITH THEM
AND WE BECAME GOOD FRIENDS;
TEBOGO AND THULI, FROM SOUTH AFRICA.

ONE DAY, I WAS OUT AND ABOUT
CHECKING CHARITY SHOPS
FOR BOOKS AND RECORDS,
WHEN I BUMPED INTO "TEBZA" (TEBOGO).
I INVITED HIM ROUND TO MINE TO CHILL.
LATER, HE GOT A CALL FROM HIS MRS.
SHE HAD FINISHED WHAT SHE WAS DOING IN TOWN,
SO HE TOLD HER TO COME TO MY PLACE.

EVENTUALLY THE DOOR BELL RANG
AND I LET THULI IN...BUT SHE WAS WITH A FRIEND.
AS WE WALKED DOWN THE NARROW HALL,
I COULDN'T QUITE SEE THE FRIEND,
BUT MY SOUL WAS EAGER TO SEE HER!
MY HEART WAS POUNDING.
I THINK MY SOUL FELL IN LOVE WITH HER
BEFORE I EVEN SAW HER FACE!

IT WAS *LOVE BEFORE FIRST SIGHT* THAT NIGHT OF THE
9TH OF MAY, 2008!

OUR FIRST OUTING AS A COUPLE WAS TO SOUTHEND AIRSHOW.

THULI *TEBOGO*
(EXPECTING AZANIA) *("Tebza"/"Dave")*

2008 *2009*

WE MET UP A WEEK LATER
AND WENT ON TO HARDLY EVER BE APART!
I COULDN'T STAND BEING AWAY FROM HER.
I EVEN HATED HOW WORK KEPT US
FROM SPENDING TIME TOGETHER.

WE WERE TOGETHER AS MUCH AS POSSIBLE.
WE WERE BEST FRIENDS.
TRUE SOULMATES.
NEARLY A DECADE LATER,
I WOULD STILL WAKE UP AND GIVE THANKS
FOR ANOTHER DAY WITH MY QUEEN.
I LOVE HER WITH ALL MY HEART.
WE'VE BEEN TOGETHER IN ALL MY LIVES, I'M SURE.

I CAN'T REMEMBER WHERE
THIS PICTURE WAS TAKEN. LOL!
LOOK AT HER FACE LIGHTING UP.
EVEN ON A COLD, SNOWY DAY!
I KNEW KHABI WAS SPECIAL...AND THAT SOME DAY
I WOULD ASK HER TO BE MY WIFE.

FOR THE FIRST TIME IN MY LIFE,
I HAD FOUND SOMEONE
THAT I COULDN'T BEAR TO BE AWAY FROM.
I'M AN ONLY CHILD SO I'VE ALWAYS
BEEN QUITE HAPPY TO SPEND TIME ALONE.

SOMETIMES IN RELATIONSHIPS
I WOULD LIKE TO GET SOME TIME ALONE,
MAYBE GO CYCLING BY THE SEASIDE
TO FREE MY MIND AND SOUL.

BUT NOT NOW...NOT ANYMORE.

I WAS FREE-EST WHEN I WAS WITH KHABI.
I WAS AT HOME IN HER LIGHT.

WHEREVER I WENT, I WANTED HER WITH ME,
OTHERWISE THE EXPERIENCE WOULDN'T BE THE SAME:
THE SUNSET WOULD BE DULL.
THE DANCE WOULD BECOME A CHORE.
THE JOKE UNAMUSING.

EVERY MOMENT....MAGICAL!

EVENTUALLY SHE MOVED TO MINE FROM THE ROOM
SHE RENTED FROM A NICE GUY CALLED RICHARD.
WE WERE SO HAPPY TOGETHER.
MAAAN, SHE EVEN STARTED COLLECTING VINYL!
WHERE DID THIS GIRL COME FROM!?!
THULI AND TEBZA, NKOSI KAKULU, NEH!
(THANK YOU SO MUCH, YEAH!)

SHE'S LIKE AN ANGEL, *A REAL ANGEL.*
HONESTLY...YOU NEED TO UNDERSTAND
THE BEAUTIFUL QUALITIES OF THIS PRINCESS.
SHE IS SO THOUGHTFUL OF OTHERS,
SHE HATES/FEARS CONFRONTATION,
SHE WANTS TO HELP EVERYONE,
SHE STUDIES HER BIBLE,
SHE'S CLEVER,
SHE'S FUNNY...

...SHE'S SIMPLY PERFECT.

SHE MADE ME KNOW *TRUE LOVE*.
SHE MADE ME BE THE BEST VERSION OF ME.
SHE EVEN GOT ME INTO WRITING,
WHICH WAS A TURN UP FOR THE BOOKS, AS IT WERE,
'COS I'VE ALWAYS BEEN MORE DRAWN TO ART!

JUST BEFORE WE MET,
KHABI LOST HER DAD, "BABA", IN SOUTH AFRICA
(WHO WAS HER STEP-DAD FROM A YOUNG AGE, TOO),
BUT HE SADLY DIED WHILE SHE WAS HERE IN THE UK.
SHE WASN'T ABLE TO ATTEND HIS FUNERAL,
WHICH WAS REALLY TROUBLING HER.

SO I TOLD HER HOW I DIDN'T BELIEVE IN DEATH
AND SHARED MY BELIEFS ABOUT ETERNAL LIFE,
LIKE HOW THE NATURE OF THE SPIRIT REALM
ALLOWS ONE TO BE IN TWO PLACES AT ONCE,
MEANING THAT IT DIDN'T MATTER
THAT SHE COULDN'T BE AT THE FUNERAL,
AS HE WAS PROBABLY HERE WITH HER
AS WELL AS BEING WITH THE FAMILY IN AFRICA.

WHEN I TOLD HER THIS AND SHARED WITH HER
ALL THE SIGNS MY DAD HAD SHOWN
SINCE HE LEFT THE FLESH,
SHE TOLD ME I HAD TO WRITE A BOOK.
SO I DID; "THE COMFORTER",
BY JUDAH JAH LOVE (MY RASTAFARI NAME),
BASED ON THESE SIGNS
AND OTHER REVELATIONS I'VE HAD.

I ASKED KHABI IF SHE'D HAD ANY DREAMS
OF HER DAD SINCE HE'D PASSED OVER. SHE HADN'T.
THEN ONE OF THE FOLLOWING DAYS
WAS FATHER'S DAY, SO I SUGGESTED SHE BRING
FLOWERS FOR HER DAD TO MY DAD'S GRAVE
WHERE WE COULD LAY FLOWERS
FOR BOTH OUR DADS, KNOWING THEY'D SEE.

WE DID THAT AND THE NEXT DAY,
KHABI SAID SHE'D DREAMT OF BABA THAT NIGHT!!!
SHE TOLD ME HE PUT HIS HAND ON HER SHOULDER
AND JUST SMILED AT HER.
SHE SAID IT COMFORTED HER
AND WAS ENOUGH TO LET HER KNOW THAT
WHERE HE IS NOW....HE'S OK!

THE SUMMER THAT FOLLOWED WAS EXTRA SPECIAL
WITH RADIANCE SHINING IN MY LIFE.

THE HAPPIEST TIME OF MY LIFE
CAME AFTER THE WORST TIME OF MY LIFE.
MEETING HER MADE SENSE OF ALL THE PAIN
OF LOSING MY DAD, BECAUSE,
IF I HADN'T MOVED BACK TO SOUTHEND
WHEN HE LEFT ME HIS FLAT,
WE MAY NEVER HAVE MET.

THANKS FOR THE GIFTS DAD!

WHEN LOVE IS TRUE, THE WHOLE WORLD CAN SEE THE HAPPINESS WITHIN:

ABOVE WAS MY 30TH BIRTHDAY OUTING, TO CHESSINGTON, 2008.

THIS WAS AFTER KHABI'S 23RD BIRTHDAY OUTING, TO SEE "THE LION KING", 2008.

CHAPTER 3...BACK TO AFRICA

WHEN KHABI'S VISA TO STAY IN THE UK RAN OUT, IT WAS A NO BRAINER...I WAS GOING WITH HER. THERE WAS ABSOLUTELY NO WAY I COULD SPEND A SINGLE DAY WITHOUT HER, SO WE WENT TO HER HOME TOGETHER.

(SOUTH AFRICA'S REAL NAME...) AZANIA, HERE WE COME!

GOING TO SOUTH AFRICA WAS AMAZING!
KHABI'S FAMILY WENT ALL OUT FOR ME
AND MADE ME FEEL SO WELCOME!
PLUS, KHABI GOT TO CATCH UP WITH FRIENDS
AND FAMILY THAT SHE HADN'T SEEN FOR YEARS.

OUS TINY, MA NONKY, MALUME MBIX ("Uncle")

COUSIN JACOB, FRIEND KAMO, NIECE KAMO

THOSE WERE SPECIAL TIMES, BUT,
BEFORE I KNEW IT, I HAD TO RETURN TO THE UK.
IT WOULD BE TWO MONTHS
BEFORE I WOULD SEE HER AGAIN.
IT WAS EXCRUTIATING. IT FELT LIKE YEARS.
I DON'T KNOW HOW MANY CALL CARDS I USED
TO KEEP IN TOUCH WITH HER EVERY DAY!

THEN, ONE DAY, I WENT ON A MISSION...
...AND BOUGHT A BEAUTIFUL ENGAGEMENT RING,
MADE ESPECIALLY FOR HER.
WHEN I BROUGHT THE RING HOME
(REMEMBER, HOME WAS MY DAD'S OLD FLAT)
I PRESSED THE BUTTON IN THE LIFT
AND IT LIT UP....WHICH WAS STRANGE...

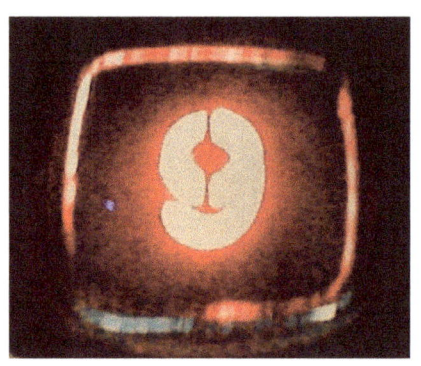

...BECAUSE IT NEVER USED TO WORK!
THERE WAS ONLY ONE OTHER TIME,
NEARLY A YEAR PRIOR,
THAT I REMEMBER THAT BUTTON LIGHTING UP!
IT WAS UPON RETURNING HOME FROM THE CEMETERY,
HAVING CELEBRATED MY DAD'S BIRTHDAY,
ON CHRISTMAS EVE,
WITH MY MUM AND KHABI,
WITH MUSIC, INCENSE AND PRAYER.
IT WAS LIKE HE WAS THANKING US.

SO WHEN IT LIT UP THIS TIME, I KNEW...
...IT WAS MY DAD GIVING US HIS BLESSING!

I WAS SOOOO NERVOUS,
CARRYING THE RING ON THE FLIGHT BACK TO HER.
IT WAS REALLY BUMPY 'N' I THOUGHT, "IF WE CRASH,
SHE'LL NEVER KNOW I WANTED TO MARRY HER!"

THEN *WOOOOOOW!*
MEETING UP WITH HER, FINALLY...
...THE AIR WAS ELECTRIC! LIKE AN OLD MOVIE SCENE.
IT WAS EMOTIONAL AND EXHILARATING!
I'LL NEVER FORGET IT.
I'D BEEN MISSING HER SO, SO MUCH.
NOW WE WERE TOGETHER AGAIN...
...THE PAIN WAS GONE.
AS SOON AS WE GOT HOME AND SETTLED...

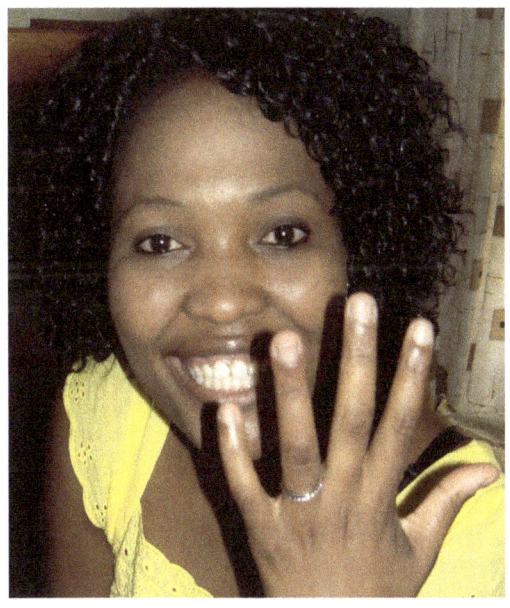

...I PROPOSED.

TWO YEARS AND TWO DAYS AFTER MEETING,
I MARRIED MY QUEEN IN JOHANNESBURG,
MAY 11TH, 2010.

MA, NONKY

MUM, SANDY

NIECE, KAMO

BROTHER, LEFA
("Skuchupunch")

WE CONTINUED ENJOYING BEING IN AFRICA, AND LOVED SPENDING TIME WITH FAMILY.

BIG BROTHER KGUWI ("Biggie!")

SISTER THANDI & NIECE, THANDO

THEN WE BOUGHT A DOG, KALI/CARLY,
A DALMATION-POINTER-CROSS PUPPY,
WHO WAS TO BECOME KHABI'S BEST BUDDY.

SADLY, THINGS DIDN'T WORK OUT HOW
WE WANTED IN SOUTH AFRICA, DUE TO THE FACT
THAT THE WHITE PEOPLE THERE, THE "AFRIKAANERS",
MAKE SURE THAT IT IS VIRTUALLY IMPOSSIBLE
FOR ANYONE OF COLOUR TO SUCCEED.

TO THIS DAY, EVEN THOUGH THEY SAY
APARTHEID IS OVER, THE REALITY IS,
MANY BLACK WOMEN WILL BECOME MAIDS
AND MANY BLACK MEN
WILL ONLY GET TO DO MANUAL LABOUR JOBS.

YOU WILL SEE MINI BUSES RUNNING AROUND,
DROPPING OFF WHOLE BUNCHES OF MAIDS,
IN THEIR DEMEANING, FRILLLY APRONS.

COMMERCIAL "BUKKIES" (OPEN-BACK VANS)
BEING DRIVEN BY THE COMPANY'S WHITE OWNERS
WITH A COUPLE OF BLACK GUYS,
VERY DANGEROUSLY SAT IN THE OPEN BACK,
HURTLING DOWN THE MOTORWAY,
LOOKING BACK AT YOU,
WITH EYES THAT JUST SAY,
"EISSSSHHHH!"

WE SAW A GARDENER, USING SCISSORS,
TO CUT THE GRASS AROUND THE PAVING STONES...
...ON CHRISTMAS DAY!
WE SAW A WAITER GET KICKED
IN FRONT OF EVERYONE, BY THE WHITE MANAGER,
JUST BECAUSE HE FORGOT PART OF THE ORDER!

THE FACT IS....APARTHEID IS FAR FROM OVER.

SO WE CAME BACK TO ENGLAND.
WE WERE HAPPY TO BE BACK,
YET SAD TO LEAVE THE FAMILY BEHIND.

WE WERE SHELL SHOCKED FROM
ALL OUR TRAVELLING AND EXPERIENCES.
WE HAD FACED CLASS 'A' RACISM,
BATTLED WITH ILLNESS AND STRESS
AND NOW WE WERE BACK WHERE WE STARTED,
JUST COMPLETELY BROKE THIS TIME.
IT WAS ALL A BIT MIND-BLOWING!

IT ALL GAVE ME TERRIBLE ANXIETY AND
I FELT FAINT GOING TO JOB INTERVIEWS,
BUT WE GOT JOBS IN SUPPORT AGAIN
AND GRADUALLY GOT BACK
INTO THE SWING OF THINGS.

WE WERE DOING WELL, GETTING PAID WELL
FOR JOBS WE ENJOYED DOING.
EVEN THOUGH IT WAS VERY HARD,
WORKING WITH EX ADDICTS
AND MENTAL PATIENTS,
WE ENJOYED KEEPING THEM WELL AND HAPPY.

WE WERE VERY HAPPY
AND, AFTER SPENDING A FORTUNE ON VISAS
AND RENEWALS OF VISAS AND EXAMS,
KHABI GOT HER FULL LEAVE TO REMAIN IN UK!

BUT THERE WAS ANOTHER REASON TO CELEBRATE...
...WE WERE EXPECTING A BABY!!!

*THIS WAS WHEN WE FOUND OUT
WE WERE WITH CHILD*

KHABI WROTE THE FOLLOWING POEM ABOUT
MY PRAYER FOR A CHILD, THE NAMES WE CAME UP WITH
AND THE JOY OF THE SCAN DATES:

KARA BOPHELO ASHENAFI ABREY

OVERWHELMING JOY FLOODED MY WHOLE BEING
THE MOMENT YOUR SPIRIT CHOSE US
JAH LOVE SAID A PRAYER AS YOU WERE CONCEIVED
GIVING THANKHS N PRAISE TO THE MOST HIGH
& THE HIGHEST CREATOR
GOD N GODDESS
FOR THE PRECIOUS GIFT OF NEW LIFE
- BOPHELO -
BESTOWED UPON US.

ON
7TH OF 12TH MONTH
THRU MODERN TEGHNOLOGY
WE LISTENED TO YOUR HEART BEAT
IT REMINDED ME OF THE DRUM BEAT
IN THE LAND OF THE RISING SUN

THE NUBIAN SOUNDS OF KA & RA
RESONATED WITHIN ME
REPRESENTING THE INFINITE
SPIRIT OF THE RISING SUN.

AND TO YOUR FATHER
THE SYMBOL OF THE ANKH
INFINITE LIFE
HE SAID YOU ARE
ASHENAFI
A MIGHTY CONQUEROR
YOU ARE THE PERFECT SYMBOL
OF THE SPECIAL UNION BETWEEN LOVE, LIGHT N BLISS
ETERNITY HAS BLESSED US WITH PURE BEING
KARA BOPHELO ASHENAFI
A GIFT OF UNITY.

16TH OF 2ND MONTH
A STRONG BEAUTIFUL PRINCESS IS WITH US
NO WORDS CAN DESCRIBE THAT
PRICELESS MOMENT
THANKH YOU FOR CHOOSING US

BOKHABINYANA (RADIANCE LOVELIGHT)

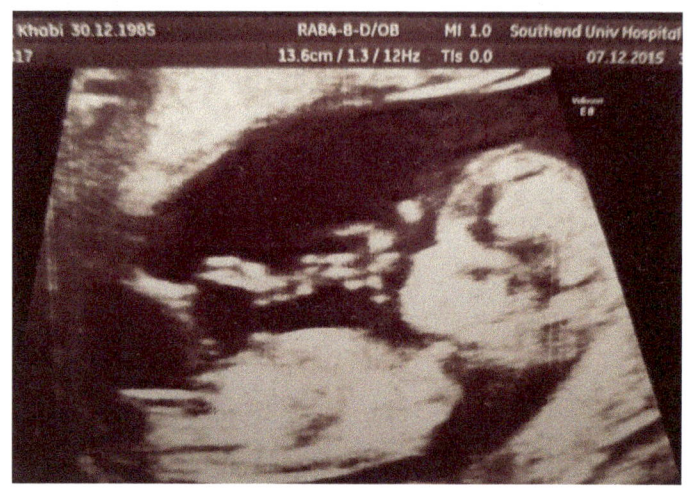

THIS IS THE FIRST SCAN OF KaRa!

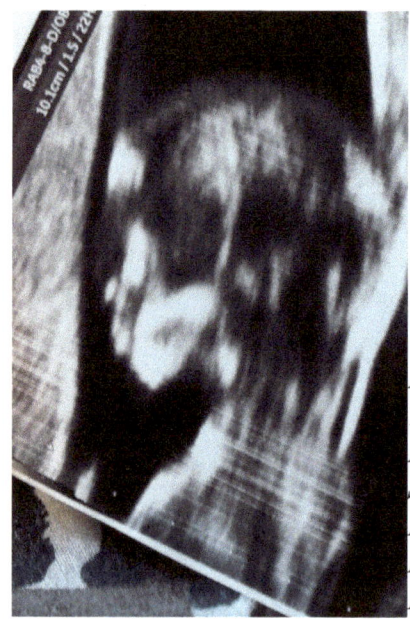

HERE, I'VE TURNED A PICTURE ON ITS SIDE, TO CREATE KaRa'S FIRST PORTRAIT!

X X

CHAPTER 4...DEATH AT THE DOOR

KaRa'S DUE DATE WAS JUNE 20TH, 2016.

EVERYTHING WAS GOING PERFECTLY.
THEN WE GOT SACKED! GREAT!
BUT WE REMAINED POSITIVE.

BY THEN,
I'D HAD SOME COPIES OF MY PREVIOUS BOOK PRINTED
AND A DANCE WAS COMING UP, BY THE SEAFRONT,
WHERE I'D BE ABLE TO TRY TO SELL SOME COPIES.

IT WAS A BIG DANCE WITH VETERAN
ROOTS REGGAE SELECTOR, "FATMAN".
WE NEEDED ALL THE MONEY WE COULD GET
AND THIS WAS A GOOD OPPORTUNITY,
SO, FOR MANY REASONS,
WE WERE EXCITED ABOUT THE NIGHT.

BY THEN, THOUGH,
KHABI WAS 8 MONTHS PREGNANT,
SO SHE RESTED IN THE DAY,
TO BE READY FOR THE EVENING.

THAT DAY WE WENT THROUGH MY ART WORK.
ONE PICTURE IN PARTICULAR, SHE LOVES.
SHE ASKED IF SHE COULD HAVE IT.
I SAID, "OF COURSE YOU CAN!".

SHE JUST LOOKED AT IT....AND CRIED.

IT WAS A CHARCOAL DRAWING I'D DONE
YEARS AGO IN LONDON,
OF THE PREGNANT WOMAN
MENTIONED IN THE BOOK OF REVELATION.

"IS THIS MY ANNIVERSARY PRESENT?",
SHE ASKED ME, AS IT WAS
TWO DAYS BEFORE OUR 8TH ANNIVERSARY.
"NO, I'LL GET YOU SOMETHING ELSE FOR THAT...
...THIS IS YOUR PREGNANCY PRESENT!"

I COOKED STEAMED VEG WITH RICE AND PEAS
AND KHABI HAD ASKED FOR A MELON,
'COS SHE LOVES HER FRUIT!
[ESPECIALLY MANGOES!
SHE SAID WHEN SHE WAS A CHILD,
SHE'D SCRAPE OFF EVERY BIT OF FLESH
FROM IT WITH HER TEETH, THEN DRY IT OUT.
IT WOULD SPLIT OPEN AS IT DRIED,
SO THE KIDS USED TO MAKE PURSES FROM THEM,
OPENING AND SHUTTING THEM WITH A SQUEEZE.]

LATER THAT EVENING, WE WERE ABOUT TO
LEAVE FOR THE DANCE, BUT,
KHABI SAID SHE DIDN'T WANT TO GO.
SHE SAID SHE FELT TOO TIRED.

I BEGGED HER TO CHANGE HER MIND,
BUT SHE HAD DECIDED TO STAY HOME
AND THAT WAS THAT.
BESIDES, I THOUGHT SHE'D BE SAFER AT HOME.

THE DANCE WAS GREAT!
I SOLD A COUPLE OF BOOKS
AND SOME JEWELLERY I'D MADE.
MEANWHILE, I KEPT IN TOUCH WITH KHABI VIA TEXT.

FATMAN PLAYED A BEAUTIFUL TUNE BY BUNNY WAILER,
CALLED, "FIRE, FIRE", AND AT ABOUT 2 IN THE MORNING,
HE PLAYED ANOTHER BEAUTIFUL TUNE BY IJAHMAN.
I WAS ROCKING AND SMILING. ALL WAS VERY WELL!

WHEN THE TUNE STOPPED,
I HEARD MY PHONE RINGING.
I DIDN'T RECOGNIZE THE NUMBER
AND NEARLY IGNORED IT...
BUT I MADE MY WAY OUTSIDE TO ANSWER IT.
THE VOICE ON THE OTHER END SAID,
"HELLO IS THAT MR ABREY?
….THERE'S BEEN A FIRE AT YOUR FLAT
AND YOUR WIFE IS VERY POORLY!"

I WENT BACK IN THE DANCE IN UTTER SHOCK.
THE POLICE WERE COMING
TO TAKE ME FROM THE DANCE TO THE HOSPITAL.
I BUMPED INTO OUR FRIEND, KEETY.
I TOLD HIM….HIS FACE LOOKED HOW I FELT;
IN DISBELIEF, SHOCK
AND DESPERATE TO KNOW MORE.

I SCRAMBLED TO PACK UP MY STALL.
THE POLICE ARRIVED PROMPTLY,
THEN I WAS JUST SITTING IN SILENCE IN THE CAR,
WITH ALL SORTS RUNNING THROUGH MY HEAD,

LIKE, WHAT'S HAPPENED? HOW DID IT HAPPEN?
HOW BAD IS IT? IS SHE OK? IS KaRa OK?

I SAID TO THE COPPERS, "COME ON GUYS,
TALK TO ME...WHAT'S HAPPENNED....HOW BAD IS IT???
BUT THEY JUST SAID
THEY DIDN'T HAVE ANY DETAILS.

THAT JOURNEY FELT LIKE IT TOOK FOREVER.

FINALLY I WAS AT A&E.
MY EYES SEARCHED THE PLACE
AS I WONDERED WHAT THE HELL WAS GOING ON.
THEN THEY WHEELED HER, UNCONSCIOUS, PASSED ME.

"OH SHHIIIIT!!! WHAT THE F*CK!!!???"

HER FACE WAS *VERY* BADLY BURNED AND SWOLLEN.
I NEARLY FAINTED SO I FOUND A CORNER
AND JUST CROUCHED ON THE FLOOR.
I WAS IN COMPLETE SHOCK...
...AND HORROR.

IT FELT LIKE I'D JUST TAKEN
A HEAVY PUNCH TO THE FACE.
AND THE STOMACH.
AND MY HEART
AND MIND.

THE DIZZINESS, SICKNESS AND CONFUSION
WAS OVERWHELMING!

IT WAS LIKE SOMETHING ON THE NEWS ON TELLY.

IT WAS THE MOST AWFUL SIGHT I'D EVER SEEN.
NO HORROR MOVIE; NO SPECIAL EFFECTS
COULD *EVER* COME CLOSE TO THIS.

[OH BABE, I'M *SO SORRY* THIS HAPPENED TO YOU!
<u>I *WISH* I'D BEEN THERE FOR YOU</u>!]

*

SHE WAS UNCONSCIOUS AND FULL OF TUBES.
THEY HAD CLEANED HER UP UPON ARRIVAL,
BUT EACH TIME I STROKED HER HAIR,
MY HANDS GOT COATED IN SOOT.
WHEN I WENT TO KISS HER HEAD,
ALL I COULD SMELL WAS FUEL.
IT'S SOUL-DESTROYING TO SEE
SOMEONE SO PRECIOUS
IN *SUCH* A BAD WAY.

THEN I HAD TO CALL MY MUM.
I SOOO DIDN'T WANT TO TELL HER.
WHAT WOULD I SAY? HOW WOULD SHE BE?
I WAS DREADING MAKING THE CALL,
I DIDN'T WANT TO SCARE HER SO MUCH
THAT SHE'D BE UNSAFE DRIVING OVER,
HOWEVER, I NEEDED HER TO BE PREPARED,
LONG BEFORE SHE GOT THERE,
THAT THIS WAS *SERIOUS*.

I THOUGHT OH GOD....MUM LOVES HER SO MUCH
AND SHE'S ALREADY BEEN THROUGH SO MUCH!

...HOW WILL SHE COPE, ESPECIALLY AFTER
EVERYTHING SHE WENT THROUGH WITH MY DAD!?!
I CALLED HER LATER THAT MORNING.
IT WAS AWFUL HEARING HER VOICE BECOME SHAKEY.
THEN I HAD TO CALL KHABI'S FAMILY IN AFRICA.
I PUT THEM ON LOUDSPEAKER AND PUT THE PHONE
TO HER EAR SO THEY COULD SPEAK TO HER,
HOPING SHE MIGHT HEAR THEM.
IT WAS HEART-BREAKING
SEEING HER LYING THERE, TOTALLY UNRESPONSIVE.

THEN I HAD TO CALL ALL HER FRIENDS.
IT WAS HARROWING RE-TELLING IT ALL,
OVER AND OVER,
HEARING EVERYONE GO INTO SHOCK,
THEN SADNESS, THEN THE QUESTIONS CAME.

MY FRIENDS WERE SO SUPPORTIVE THOUGH.
MY BREDRINS, JASON AND SHAUN RUSHED DOWN
FROM LONDON TO THE HOSPITAL, IMMEDIATELY.
NO SUPRISE THOUGH...
...THEY'VE *ALWAYS* BEEN THERE FOR ME,
WITH BROTHERLY LOVE, GUIDANCE
AND SPIRITUAL MEDITATIONS
BLESS YOU BOTH, *TRULY!*

KHABI'S FRIEND, SHERLEY, DROVE FOR HOURS
FROM SUSSEX WITH HER TWO SMALL CHILDREN
TO BE AT THE HOSPITAL, TOO.
SHE CALLED HER PASTOR TO PRAY FOR KHABI.
IT WAS SUCH A SAD AND DESPERATE SCENE.
SHERLEY WAS CRYING AS SHE HELD THE
PHONE OVER KHABI, WITH THE PASTOR
ON LOUDSPEAKER PRAYING IN TONGUES,
WHICH I'M NOT PERSONALLY A FAN OF,
BUT I WAS AS DESPERATE AS EVERYONE ELSE WAS
AND WILLING TO LET ANYONE TRY *ANY*THING!

THIS IS THE PASTOR,
"(talking in tongues).....SHE WILL NOW WAKE UP!"
"IS THE GIRL MOVING???"

"*NO!* SHE'S *NOT MOV*IIIING!!!" SHERLEY YELLED.

JASON ALSO ASKED HIS DOCTOR,
WHO WAS VERY SPIRITUAL,
TO SEND OUT SOME HEALING.
WE DID EVERYTHING WE COULD.
WE PLAYED HER MUSIC OFF OUR PHONES.
HER FAMILY PRAYED IN THEIR LANGUAGE.
WE WERE ALL SO SCARED OF LOSING HER.
WHILE ALL THIS WAS GOING ON,
THE POLICE WERE, APPARENTLY, QUESTIONING
MY FRIENDS THAT WERE AT THE DANCE…
…TO SEE IF MY "'STORY' CHECKED OUT OK"!!!

AT 2:44 AM, ON THE 8TH OF MAY,
IT WAS CONFIRMED THAT WE HAD LOST BABY KaRa.
THEY DID AN ULTRASOUND SCAN
TO CHECK FOR ANY ACTIVITY.
IT WAS THE SADDEST SIGHT
YOU SHOULD *NEVER* SEE…
…JUST A PILE OF BONES
ON THE SCREEN.
MOTIONLESS.

I COULD FEEL MY HEART BREAK AS I STARED AT HER.

THEN….THE NEXT DAY,
THE 9TH OF MAY, 2016,
EXACTLY 8 YEARS AFTER LOVE BEFORE FIRST SIGHT,
KHABI WAS FOUND UNRESPONSIVE TO ALL TESTS.
IT WAS OVER. HER LIFE *AND* MINE, IT FELT LIKE.

SHE WAS MERELY 30 YEARS YOUNG.

THIS IS THE LAST PHOTO WE TOOK TOGETHER, TAKEN A COUPLE OF NIGHTS BEFORE THE FIRE.

I JUST STOOD THERE LOOKING AT HER,
CLUTCHING MY HEART.
I BEGGED HER TO SHOW US A MIRACLE.
IF ANYONE COULD PERFORM MIRACLES
I BELIEVED *SHE* COULD,
BUT NO SUCH THING HAPPENED...
...MAYBE FOR THE BEST...
...HER HEART HAD STOPPED BEATING
FOR *TWENTY MINUTES* AT THE SCENE,
SO SHE WOULD HAVE SUFFERED SEVERE
BRAIN DAMAGE AND HER INJURIES
WOULD HAVE BEEN UNBEARABLY PAINFUL.
TWO DAYS LATER, ON MAY 11TH,
OUR 6TH WEDDING ANNIVERSARY,
A MAN WE'D NEVER MET, *FROM THE FLAT BELOW US,*
LILLO, WAS ARRESTED FOR ARSON
AND CHILD DESTRUCTION.

<u>HE WAS A PARANOID SCHIZOPHRENIC</u>
NOT BEING CARED FOR ADEQUATELY,
WHO HAD MOVED IN BELOW US A YEAR BEFORE.
<u>HE WAS ALSO A *CONVICTED* ARSONIST.</u>

HE BELIEVED THAT THE INCREDIBLY LOUD MUSIC
BEING PLAYED ALL THROUGH MANY NIGHTS
'TIL 5/7AM WAS COMING FROM US.
YES, WE PLAYED TUNES NOW AND THEN,
BUT NOT *THAT* LOUD AND NOT *THAT* LATE.
IT WAS COMING FROM A FLAT ABOVE US
AND HE COULD HEAR IT BELOW US,
THAT'S HOW LOUD IT WAS.

HE'D BEEN STRUGGLING
WITH HIS MENTAL HEALTH
AND'D HAD A VOICE IN HIS HEAD
TELLING HIM TO SET FIRE TO OUR FLAT,
TO SCARE US INTO MOVING OUT.

SMOKE CAME THROUGH OUR FIRE DOOR
AND FILLED THE WHOLE FLAT IN MINUTES!
THE ALARM WAS RAISED AT 11:11PM
AND CREWS ARRIVED AROUND 11:17 PM,
BUT BY THEN, THE SMOKE HAD TRAVELLED,
DOWN OUR HALL, ENTERED OUR BEDROOM,
FILLED THE ROOM WITH ENOUGH SMOKE
TO COVER KHABI'S HANDS IN SOOT,
MAKING HER LEAVE HAND MARKS
AS SHE STRUGGLED OUT OF BED,
HAVING BEEN WOKEN UP BY THE SMOKE.

THERE WERE HANDPRINTS
ALL OVER THE WINDOW FRAME
FROM WHERE **SHE'D FRANTICALLY TRIED
TO OPEN THE WINDOW FOR AIR, BUT ALAS,
IN HER PANIC, SHE COULDN'T UNDO THE CHILD
RESTRICTORS, SO SHE *HAD* TO FLEE THE FLAT...
...INTO THE FIRE**. SHE BANGED ON DOORS
SHOUTING FOR HELP...BUT
IN THE THICK, TOXIC SMOKE,
SHE ONLY HAD SECONDS.

MY SUNSHINE WAS GONE
IN MOMENTS.

SOMEONE DID TRY TO SAVE HER!
RICHARD, WHO LIVES A FEW FLOORS ABOVE US,
BUT HE WAS TOO LATE...AND NEARLY DIED
IN THE PROCESS! BLESS YOU BROTHER! YOU TRIED!
THANK YOU, THANK YOU, *THANK YOU!*

CHAPTER 5...THE AFTERMATH

WHEN I FIRST WENT BACK TO THE FLAT,
I WASN'T PREPARED FOR THIS NEXT SHOCKING SIGHT...
COMING OUT OF THE LIFT I WAS HIT BY WHAT I SAW.
EVERY INCH OF THE CORRIDOOR WALLS AND CEILING
WERE TOTALLY BLACK AND THE SILVER METAL
WAS SHOWING THROUGH ON THE FRONT DOORS.

THIS PHOTO WAS TAKEN AFTER *EXTENSIVE* CLEANING
HAD BEEN DONE...BUT, SEE HOW BLACK
THE WHITE WALLS ARE, BETWEEN - AND RUNNING
ACROSS THE TOP OF - THE TWO END DOORS,
WELL IMAGINE *ALL* THE WALLS *AND* CEILING
IN THIS PICURE - AND FAR BEYOND -
WERE AS BLACK AS THAT, WITH THE FLOOR
HAVING ONLY PATCHES OF GREEN SHOWING!
IT WAS LIKE IT WAS DARK, BUT YOU COULD SEE PERFECTLY!

IT WAS SHOCKINGLY DIFFERENT
FROM HOW I KNEW IT TO LOOK.
EVERYTHING LOOKED UNFAMILIAR,
LIKE A MOVIE SET RATHER THAN MY HOME.
I FELT LIKE I'D GONE TO THE WRONG PLACE.

PEOPLE WERE CLEANING THE WALLS.
THERE WAS POLICE TAPE OVER MY OPEN FLAT DOOR
AND FOOTPRINTS IN FUEL ALL OVER THE FLOOR,
ESPECIALLY OUTSIDE OUR DOOR AND BY THE LIFT...
WHERE KHABI WAS FOUND. I FELT SO MANY EMOTIONS.
OUR DOOR WAS OPEN. IT COULDN'T CLOSE PROPERLY
'COS THE PLASTIC FRAMES WERE SO BADLY MELTED!
ANYONE COULD'VE GONE IN! AND THEY HAD!

THE FIRE BRIGADE HAD (QUITE RIGHTLY)
RANSACKED THE PLACE LOOKING FOR ANY
HIDDEN CHILDREN/PEOPLE IN THE FLAT.
BUT THE POLICE HAD ALSO SEARCHED THE FLAT.
OUR CUPBOARDS HAD BEEN RIFLED THROUGH
AND OUR CAMERA, WITH ALL OUR PRIVATE MOMENTS
HAD BEEN SCRUTINIZED, AS I WAS ASKED ABOUT
A VIDEO I'D MADE OF THE FLATS' DRY-RISER,
AS IT'D BEEN MAKING A TERRIBLE NOISE.

I WALKED INTO THE FLAT FEELING ZOMBIFIED.
GREASEY SOOT WAS *EVERYWHERE!*
IN EVERY ROOM, IN EVERY CUPBOARD,
IN THE WARDROBES, ALL OVER OUR CLOTHES,
OUR RECORDS, OUR BOOKS, OUR PLATES,
THE CARPET, THE SOFA, THE CEILINGS AND CURTAINS!

THERE WAS SOOT IN OUR BED
AND ALL OVER THE COT.
OH MAAANNN! SUCH SAD SIGHTS!
[AWWWW KaRa! I WAS *SOOO* LOOKING FORWARD
TO MEETING YOU AND HOLDING YOU!]

I FOUND MYSELF JUST STANDING IN THE LOUNGE,
IN A COMPLETE DAZE.
THEN A LADY WHO HAD BEEN OUTSIDE,
CLEANING THE WALL IN THE HALLWAY
APPEARED AT THE LOUNGE DOOR.
SHE JUST CAME IN AND HUGGED ME.
SHE SAID I LOOKED IN A BAD WAY
AS I WENT FROM THE LIFT TO MY FLAT,
AND THOUGHT I COULD DO WITH A HUG.
SPOT ON, BLESS HER!

THEN I WENT IN THE KITCHEN
AND OPENED THE FRIDGE
ONLY TO FIND THE MELON I'D BOUGHT FOR KHABI.
IT HAD SEVERAL SLICES MISSING.
IT MUST'VE BEEN THE LAST THING SHE EVER ATE.

IT WAS ALL IMMENSLY SAD AND SHOCKING.
PAIN WAS PILING UP ON MORE PAIN.
I FELT LIKE A BALLOON EXPANDING TO ITS LIMITS.

MY WORLD HAD BEEN INVADED AND DESTROYED,
ALL WHILE I WAS OUT, JUST 5 MINUTES DOWN THE ROAD.
I FELT SICK AND HOLLOW...*LITERALLY GUTTED.*
WE HAD SO MUCH AHEAD OF US.

I STAYED AT MY MUM'S FLAT
IN THE WEEKS IMMEDIATELY AFTER THE INCIDENT
(I DIDN'T GO BACK TO THE FLAT UNTIL
FRIENDS AND FAMILY ARRIVED FROM AFRICA
FOR THE FUNERAL). IT WAS A TERRIBLE TIME.
SLEEPING WAS ACTUALLY EASY, IT WAS WAKING UP
WHEN THE FUN AND GAMES STARTED.
THERE'D BE ABOUT 5-10 SECONDS
WHERE I WAS JUST AWARE OF WAKING UP ALL COZY,
THEN THE REALIZATION OF THE REALITY
WOULD DESCEND UPON ME.

MY FACE WOULD START TO TINGLE AND GO NUMB.
THEN I WOULD GET THIS SORT OF
FLASHING FEELING ON MY FACE
AND THUMPING ON MY CHEST,
IT WAS HORRENDOUS.
IT HAPPENED EVERY DAY.
OVER AND OVER AND OVER AND OVER.
BREATHLESS. SWEATING. SHAKING.
FEELING FAINT AND NAUSEAUS.
MORNING AFTER MORNING WITHOUT FAIL.
I GUESS THAT'S WHY THEY CALL IT MOURNING,
BECAUSE IT HURTS THE WORST IN THE MORNING.

IT GOT TO THE STAGE WHERE
I WOULD WAKE UP AND THINK,
"OH GOD, HERE WE GO AGAIN",
ALMOST WISHING I WOULD STOP WAKING UP
TO ESCAPE THE REPETITIVE AGONY.

I WOULD START TO FEEL SICK, SO I WOULD RUSH TO THE SINK AND HEAVE, BUT NOTHING EVER CAME UP... BUT THE TEARS CAME DOWN.

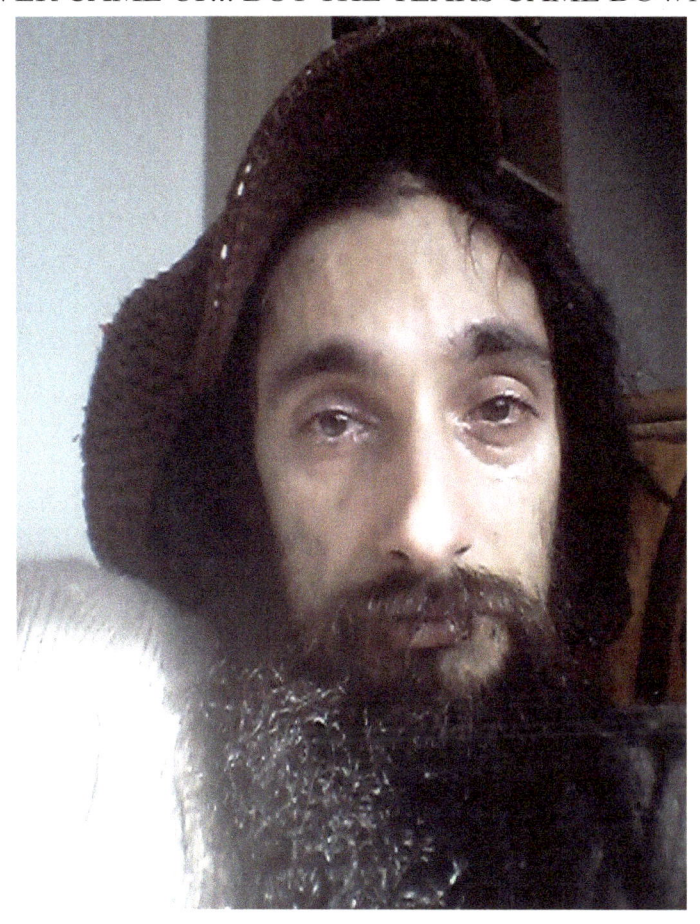

SHOULDERS UP WITH TENSION, EXTRA-SKINNY AND SLUMPED IN EMOTIONAL EXHAUSTION, SITTING WHERE I SAT EACH DAY...STARING INTO SPACE... ...THINKING...CRYING...SOMETIMES SCREAMING.

ONE TIME I CRIED SO HARD
I NEARLY PASSED OUT.
I COULDN'T TAKE A BREATH IN.
IT WAS JUST ONE LONG OUT-BREATH OF AGONY.
I CROUCHED TO THE FLOOR OUT OF WEAKNESS.
IT WAS SCARY...I THOUGHT I WASN'T GONNA BE ABLE
TO BREATHE IN AGAIN...I THOUGHT I MIGHT DIE!
IT WAS LIKE A LIVING NIGHTMARE.
QUITE LITERALLY....IT WAS *MURDER!*

SOMETIMES, CRYING TURNED TO SCREECHING.
IT MADE ME SHUDDER HEARING MYSELF...
…'COS I'D HEARD THE SOUND BEFORE...
...IT WAS THE SOUND LILLO WAS MAKING
DURING HIS BREAKDOWN.

SUDDENLY I FELT A CONNECTION WITH HIM.
I KNOW **WE ARE *ALL* CONNECTED**
AND THIS WAS EVIDENCE OF THAT.
HE WAS ME...I WAS NOW HIM.
HE HAD TRANSFERRED HIS AGONY TO ME.
NOW *I* WAS IN *HIS* MENTAL HELL.

I FELT SICK ALL THE TIME.
MY BODY ACHED.
JUST WALKING AROUND
WAS DRAINING AND AWKWARD.
I WAS WORN OUT FROM WITHIN.
IT NOW FELT LIKE I WAS SUDDENLY
IN A TOTALLY DIFFERENT REALITY
FROM EVERYONE ELSE.

ONE DAY I WAS IN TOWN FOR SOME REASON,
AND SOMEONE GOES TO ME,
"AIN'T YOU (H)'OT?"
IT WAS A BOILING HOT, SUNNY DAY
AND I WAS IN A THICK HOODIE.
IT WAS A GORGEOUS DAY 'N' I HADN'T EVEN NOTICED!
I FELT LIKE THE LIVING DEAD ALL DAY,
UNTIL THE EVENING, WHEN I WOULD BEGIN
TO FEEL A BIT MORE NORMAL,
WHICH I CHERISHED, SO I WOULD STAY UP LATE
TO ENJOY NOT FEELING ILL.

THE BODY SEEMS TO KEEP TRACK OF TIME.
WHEN IT GETS CLOSE TO THE ANNIVERSARY,
SOMEHOW MY BODY KNOWS WHAT THE DATE IS,
EVEN BEFORE I DO! FOR EXAMPLE, AS I WRITE THIS,
IT'S APRIL 3RD, 2021 AND FOR 3 DAYS
I'VE BEEN HAVING STOMACH PAINS
AND AN UPSET STOMACH.
I'VE BEEN STRUGGLING TO EAT,
EVEN IF I FEEL HUNGRY,
BECAUSE I'VE GONE BACK TO FEELING SICK
AT THE THOUGHT OF EATING ANYTHING.

EVEN THOUGH I HAVEN'T BEEN THINKING
ABOUT THE DATE OR THE ANNIVERSARY;
EVEN THOUGH I HAVEN'T BEEN
FEELING PARTICULARLY SAD;
EVEN THOUGH THE SUN'S BEEN SHINING,
MY BODY IS AWARE THAT THE DATE IS COMING UP.
MY BODY IS STARTING TO GET SAD,
EVEN IF MY MIND ISN'T!

I ALSO FIND THAT WHEN I FEEL LIKE THIS
AND CALL FAMILY IN SA, THEY WILL SAY
THEY ARE ALSO FEELING ILL AT THAT TIME.
SUCH A STRONG CONNECTION BETWEEN US ALL.

BECAUSE OF THE LATE NIGHTS
I WAS SLEEPING WELL INTO THE DAY,
WHICH I FOUND MEANT I'D MANAGED TO
MISS THE WINDOW OF PAIN
IN THE EARLY HOURS OF THE MOURNING.
SO I SLEPT AS MUCH AS I COULD.
THANK GOD I COULD SLEEP!
LIVING MY DAY WAS THE HARD PART.

WHEN I FELT STRONG ENOUGH,
I WOULD GO AND DO THE SHOPPING,
BUT I'D BE IN THE SUPERMARKET WITH A FACE
THAT I COULD FEEL DID NOT LOOK HAPPY.
I JUST WANTED TO CRY ALL THE TIME.
ANYWHERE, ANYTIME, CRYING COULD STRIKE.
SO I'D GRAB THE ESSENTIALS AND
GET THE HELL OUT OF THERE,
GET HOME AND OPEN THE FLOODGATES.

ALSO, I HAD STARTED TO FEEL SICK
JUST AT THE SMELL OF FOOD COOKING.
WORSE IF THE FOOD WAS BURNING!
EVEN SALAD BECAME A PROBLEM!
I FOUND THIS REALLY SCARY AS
I WAS ALREADY STICK-THIN
AND I WAS *SO* HUNGRY!

EATING WAS A NIGHTMARE AND I'VE NEVER HAD
A GREAT RELATIONSHIP WITH FOOD AS IT IS.
THE ONLY FOOD THAT DIDN'T MAKE ME FEEL SICK
- NEITHER PREPARING IT NOR EATING IT -
WAS MARMITE ON TOAST!!!

I HAD TO LIGHTLY TOAST THE BREAD
TO AVOID ANY BURNING SMELLS
WHICH MIGHT TRIGGER NAUSEA, BUT,
THERE WAS NOTHING ABOUT THE TASTE
OR THE TEXTURE OF THE MARMITE
THAT CAUSED ANY PROBLEMS.
THE THICKER IT WAS SPREAD THE BETTER!
BECAUSE I DIDN'T HAVE A TOASTER,
I WAS GRILLING THE BREAD IN THE OVEN
AND DISCOVERED THAT
PUTTING THE TOAST BACK UNDER THE GRILL,
AFTER PUTTING THE MARMITE ON THE TOAST
GAVE IT AN EVEN NICER TASTE AND TEXTURE.

EVEN SO, IT WAS STILL A STRUGGLE TO EAT...
...AS MY EYES KEPT FILLING UP WITH TEARS.
CHEWING WAS SLOW AND SWALLOWING
WAS HARD TO DO WHILE CRYING.

MY MUM WAS A STAR,
HAVING ME ROUND FOR DINNER EACH NIGHT,
SAVING ME FROM THE FEAR AND ANXIETY
BROUGHT ON AT THE THOUGHT OF GOING SHOPPING,
NOT KNOWING WHAT I SHOULD BUY
AND BEING TOO WEAK TO STAND TO COOK!

"IT'S AWFUL WITHOUT YOU BABE"
"CAN'T YOU COME BACK???"
"I MISS YOU SO MUCH."
*"I MISS **US!**"*

CHAPTER 6...THE THINGS PEOPLE SAY!

IT WAS HARD WORK GOING OUT, NOT ONLY BECAUSE
JUST THROWING ONE FOOT IN FRONT OF THE OTHER
USED MORE STRENGTH THAN I FELT I HAD LEFT...
...BUT ALSO BECAUSE EVERYWHERE I WENT,
I SAW PEOPLE THAT KNOW US, THAT KNEW KHABI
AND I'D HAVE TO KEEP REPEATING WHAT'D HAPPENED.

I WOULD GO FOR A CYCLE ALONG THE SEAFRONT
JUST TO BE OUT YET STILL AVOID PEOPLE.
BUT MOST OF THE TIME, HER/OUR FRIENDS
WERE EVERYWHERE I WENT AND I HAD TO
RECOUNT AND RELIVE THE WHOLE THING
OVER AND OVER AGAIN.

SOME PEOPLE TRIED TO RELATE TO WHAT HAPPENED
THE BEST THEY COULD, BY SAYING THINGS LIKE,
"AWW IT'S LIKE WHEN I LOST MY GRANNY..."
OR
"I KNOW WHAT IT WAS LIKE WHEN MY DOG DIED..."*

THIS WAS QUITE DIFFICULT TO HEAR
BEACAUSE SOMEONE BEING MURDERED
IS NOTHING LIKE A GRANNY OR A DOG DYING,
BUT I KNEW WHAT THEY WERE TRYING TO DO
AND I APPRECIATED IT.
THEY HAVE NO IDEA WHAT IT'S LIKE, BECAUSE,
THANKFULLY, NOT MANY PEOPLE HAVE LOST PEOPLE
IN AN UNTIMELY, TRAGIC AND VIOLENT MANNER.

*see notes on P. 229-30

IT SEEMS THERE ARE DIFFERENT LEVELS OF PAIN
FOR DIFFERENT SOULS BEING LOST AND
FOR DIFFERENT CIRCUMSTANCES OF THE LOSS;

LOSING A PET
IS DIFFERENT FROM LOSING A GRANDPARENT,
WHICH IS DIFFERENT FROM LOSING YOUR DAD,
WHICH IS DIFFERENT FROM LOSING YOUR MUM,
WHICH IS DIFFERENT FROM LOSING A SIBBLING,
WHICH IS DIFFERENT FROM LOSING A TWIN,
WHICH IS DIFFERENT FROM LOSING A BABY,
WHICH IS DIFFERENT FROM LOSING A GROWN CHILD,
WHICH IS DIFFERENT FROM LOSING YOUR PARTNER.

AND; LOSING SOMEONE DUE TO OLD AGE
IS DIFFERENT FROM IT BEING DUE TO ILLNESS,
WHICH IS DIFFERENT FROM AN ACCIDENT,
WHICH IS DIFFERENT FROM MANSLAUGHTER,
WHICH IS DIFFERENT FROM SUICIDE,
WHICH IS DIFFERENT FROM MURDER.

WHEN MY DAD DIED,
FOR ME, IT WAS ABSOLUTELY AWFULL, BUT...
...I NEVER REALIZED HOW MUCH WORSE
MY MUM MUST HAVE BEEN FEELING (FEELS),
AS LOSING A PARTNER, FOR ME AT LEAST,
SEEMS TO BE THE WORST KIND OF LOSS,
BECAUSE YOU HAVE SUCH A UNIQUE BOND,
SUCH AN INTIMATE LOVE AND
PERSONAL RELATIONSHIP.
[LOSING A CHILD COMES *DAMN* CLOSE TO IT THOUGH!]

LUCKILY MOST PEOPLE DON'T UNDERSTAND THIS
HIERARCHY OF HURT,
BUT UNFORTUNATELY, THIS MEANS
THEY MAY SAY THINGS QUITE INNOCENTLY,
WITH ALL THE RIGHT INTENTIONS,
THAT JUST *WIND YOU UP*.

GRIEF IS FUNNY THOUGH...I READ ON THE NET
WORDS TO THIS EFFECT:
SOMEONE CAN ASK YOU HOW YOU ARE
AND THIS MAKES YOU ANGRY, 'COS YOU THINK,
"HOW DO YOU THINK I FEEL!!!???" AND YET...
...YOU STILL GET MAD
IF THEY *DON'T* ASK HOW YOU ARE!?!
THAT BEING SAID,
SOME PEOPLE *REALLY DID*
HAVE SOME OFF-KEY COMMENTS TO MAKE;
SOMEONE FROM MY FLATS SAID TO ME,
"SOOO....YOU'RE WAITING FOR INSURANCE???"

"WHA' D' YOU MEAN???", I SNAPPED.

"SHE DIDN'T HAVE LIFE INSURANCE?"

THIS IS ME, "NO!"

"NO INSURANCE ON YOUR FLAT?"

"*NO!*"

"*OH!* (pauses in thought/disbelief) OK, SEE YOUU!"
'N' OFF HE WENT!!!

NO NO, DON'T SWEAR!
NOT YET ANYWAY....THINGS GET WORSE:

ONE FINE DAY, I BUMPED INTO A NICE LADY
WHO LIVED LOCALLY AND SEEMED
TO BE STRUGGLING WITH
MENTAL HEALTH ISSUES OR
A LEARNING DISABILITY,
MOST LIKELY BROUGHT ABOUT
BY THE *TERRIBLY* SAD EVENTS IN HER LIFE,
YET SHE WAS ALWAYS SMILEY
AND WE USED TO SPEAK TO HER
WHEN WE SAW HER.

SHE HAD BEEN EXCITED ABOUT THE BABY,
LIKE *EVERYONE* WAS,
AND SHE ASKED AFTER KHABI.

I TOLD HER WHAT HAD HAPPENED.
SHE JUST STOOD THERE SILENT,
LOOKING AT ME, ALMOST SCRUTINIZING ME.

THEN FINALLY SHE BREAKS
THE SILENCE AND THE TENSION WITH,
"I'M JUST SURPRISED, THAT'S ALL!"
"I MEAN ONE MINUTE YOU'RE EXPECTING A BABY...
...NOW *THIS!*"

"*I'M* SURPRISED *TOO!*" I BARKED.
THEN SHE JUST WALKED OFF, LEAVING ME
WONDERING WHAT SHE WAS DRIVING AT.

SOME DAYS LATER I SAW HER AGAIN.

"*WHY DID YOU DO IT*!?!" SHE DEMANDED.

"DO *WHAT!!!???*"

"THE PAPERS SAY YOU KILLED YOUR WIFE...
...*DID* YOU???"

AS YOU CAN IMAGINE, I WANTED TO GO MAD!

"*CAN YOU READ???*"

"YES, I CAN READ!"

"WELL GO AND READ
THAT PAPER AGAIN - PROPERLY -
AND YOU WILL SEE IT SAYS
LILLO TROISI KILLED HER!"

SHE DID AND LATER APOLOGIZED,
BUT I WAS STILL TROUBLED BY IT.
IT REALLY DISTURBED ME
THAT SOMEONE WHO KNEW ME FAIRLY WELL
COULD THINK OR BELIEVE
THAT I COULD DO ANYTHING LIKE THAT!
YES SHE MAY HAVE MIS-READ THE NEWSPAPER,
BUT I LIKE TO THINK THAT
EVEN IF THE PAPERS LIED
AND SAID THAT I *DID* KILL MY WIFE,
THAT PEOPLE WOULD RECOIL AND NOT BELIEVE IT.

I ALREADY FELT UNSAFE
- BEFORE AND AFTER THE FIRE -
BUT THIS MADE ME EXTRA WORRIED!

WHAT IF OTHER PEOPLE WERE THINKING
SOMETHING AS STUPID AS THIS!?!
WHAT IF THIS WAS MAKING PEOPLE ANGRY AT ME!?!
WHAT IF THEY WANT TO HURT OR EVEN KILL ME!?!

MY PARANOIA WENT THROUGH THE ROOF!
THE FIRE WAS AIMED AT THE WRONG PEOPLE!
(NOT THAT IT SHOULD'VE BEEN AIMED
AT ANYONE, OR EVEN DONE AT ALL!)

INNOCENT LIVES HAD ALREADY BEEN LOST.
I KEPT/ KEEP FEARING SOMETHING ELSE
HORRENDOUS MIGHT HAPPEN.
FEAR, ITSELF, MAKES YOU ILL.

I THOUGHT MY DAD TAKING HIS OWN LIFE
WOULD BE THE WORST THING
I WOULD EVER HAVE TO GO THROUGH...
...BUT *THIS*....THIS IS A WHOLE NEW REALM OF PAIN.

WHEN MY DAD "DIED", I STRUGGLED A LOT
AND BROKE DOWN CRYING ALL THE TIME,
BUT I WAS SOON ABLE TO GO BACK TO WORK
AND GOT MYSELF TOGETHER AGAIN.
BUT THIS JUST NEVER SEEMS TO LET UP.

IT GETS WORSE YOU SEE....

CHAPTER 7...A DAGGER TO THE HEART

THE NIGHT KHABI WAS PRONOUNCED DEAD,
I WAS ASKED BY THE STAFF
WHAT I WANTED DONE WITH BABY KaRa...
...DID I WANT THEM TO REMOVE HER FROM KHABI!

I TOLD THEM TO LEAVE HER WHERE SHE IS,
TO KEEP EVERYTHING NATURAL.
THEY UNDERSTOOD.

THEN THE POLICE ADVISED ME THERE WOULD
HAVE TO BE A POST MORTEM
TO ASCERTAIN THE CAUSE OF DEATH!
I SAID, "BUT IT'S OBVIOUS HOW SHE DIED...
...*YOU* TOLD ME HOW SHE DIED!"

THEY SAID THAT BY LAW THEY HAD TO RULE OUT
ANY OTHER CAUSE OF DEATH,
JUST IN CASE THE DEFENDANT
DENIED THE CHARGES!
[HE DIDN'T, BTW!]

LIKE I SAID...I MAN A *RASTA* MAN.
I&I DONT DEAL WITH CUTTING THE FLESH.
I TOLD THEM THE BIBLE SAYS
NOT TO MAKE ANY CUTTINGS IN THE FLESH.

THEY SAID IT'S THE LAW.
"YEAH...BUT *WHOSE* LAW? BESIDES, LAWS CHANGE;
ONLY A FEW YEARS AGO ALCOHOL WAS ILLEGAL!"

THEY JUST KEPT SAYING
"IT'S THE LAW!", "IT'S THE *LAW!*"
I WOULD PROBABLY UNDERSTAND THIS
UNDER DIFFERENT CIRCUMSTANCES,
BUT NOT WHEN THEY HAD SO MUCH PROOF!

I ASKED THE POLICE TO GIVE ME
THE CORONORS' PHONE NUMBER
AND I CALLED HIM DIRECTLY.
I BEGGED AND BEGGED HIM NOT TO DO IT.
I COULDN'T BEAR THE IDEA OF HER BODY
BEING TAMPERED WITH BY STRANGERS,
THAT'S *STILL* <u>MY QUEEN</u>!

I SHOULD HAVE A SAY
IN WHAT HAPPENS TO HER BODY
AND HOW IT GETS TREATED!
**I AM STILL HER
GUARDIAN AND PROTECTOR!
MY RIGHTS SHOULDN'T END WITH HER LIFE!
MY LOVE HASN'T ENDED!
I NEVER SAID, "'TIL DEATH US DO PART"...
...I SAID, *"FOREVER!"***

I HATE INJUSTICE. I'M A LEO AND
I'M STUBBORN WHEN I KNOW I'M RIGHT,
SO I CONTINUED MY CASE WITH THE CORONOR;
"WHAT ABOUT MY RELIGION!!!???"

"I'M AFRAID THE LAW STATES THAT WE HAVE TO
RULE OUT ANY OTHER POSSIBLE CAUSE OF DEATH."

"BUT IT'S OBVIOUS SHE DIED
FROM THE SMOKE AND FLAMES OF THE FIRE!
YOU'VE TOLD ME *THAT!*
I MEAN WHAT ELSE COULD BE MISSING!?!
IF SHE ACTUALLY DIED
BY HITTING HER HEAD WHEN SHE FELL,
SHE WOULD STILL HAVE FALLEN
BECAUSE OF THE SMOKE AND FLAMES!!!"

"IT'S THE LAW.", HE KEPT REPEATING.

"*PLEASE!* MAN TO MAN, I'M TELLING YOU,
I DON'T WANT THIS TO BE DONE TO HER BODY...
...AS A HUSBAND. WHAT ABOUT THAT...
...OUR RELATIONSHIP!?!
WHAT ABOUT LOVE!?!"

I TRIED MY BEST FOR MY WIFE, BUT IT WAS IN VAIN.
THE POLICE DID ASSURE ME, THOUGH,
THAT THEY HAD SPOKEN WITH THE CORONOR AND
HE HAD AGREED TO DO MINIMAL INVESTIGATION.

NOT ONLY DID THE P.M. GO AHEAD,
BUT, TO MY CONTINUING HORROR,
THEY REMOVED KaRa FROM KHABI,
SENT HER TO GREAT ORMOND STREET
HOSPITAL FOR CHILDREN...
...AND DID A POST MORTEM ON HER, TOO!!!
MY FAMILY HAD BEEN INVADED,
INSPECTED AND DISCECTED AGAINST MY WILL.
WICKED SYSTEM! *VAM-PYRE!*

THEY MAKE YOU THINK YOU'RE FREE
TO CONTROL YOUR DESTINY, BUT YOU'RE NOT!
AT THE VERY END OF THE DAY
YOU WILL BELONG TO THEM
AND THEY WILL DO WHATEVER THEY WANT!
I APPROACHED THE POLICE, ASKING FOR
ALL THE NOTES AND ALL THE SAMPLES
THAT HAD BEEN TAKEN, DURING THE POST-MORTEM,
INCLUDING PIECES OF THE WOMB AND PLACENTA.
THEY AGREED TO HELP, BUT THERE WAS SILENCE.
I CHASED IT UP. THEY APOLOGISED 'N' TOLD ME,
"NOBODY USUALLY ASKS WHAT YOU'RE ASKING."

AFTER MORE WAITING, I PHONED THE HOSPITAL
AND - AFTER EVEN MORE WAITING,
RESPONSES AND REPEATED ENQUIRIES -
I GOT ALL THE HOSPITAL NOTES,
FROM SOUTHEND AND GT.ORMOND ST.
REGARDING ADMITTANCE, CARE, DEATH
AND POST MORTEM NOTES.

THE BODY SAMPLES TAKEN FROM KHABI AND KaRa
HAD BEEN SENT SEPERATELY TO THE FUNERAL HOME,
FROM WHENCE I HAD TO COLLECT THEM.
THAT WAS A TOUGH DAY FOR ME.
I WANTED TO HAVE ALL THEIR SAMPLES BACK,
IN THE SAME WAY WE WERE GOING TO KEEP
KaRa'S UMBILICAL CHORD AND PLACENTA,
BECAUSE THOSE THINGS ARE PART OF YOU
AND SHOULD BE TREATED WITH RESPECT,
RATHER THAN DISCARDED OR "BAD-MINDED".

I WAS PLEASED TO GET THEM BACK,
BUT IT WAS STILL A VERY SOLEMN MOMENT.
IT FELT LIKE IT WAS THEIR
WHOLE BODY BEING COLLECTED.
THEY WILL BE BURIED WHEN I FINALLY
SORT OUT THE HEADSTONE...
...OR THEY'LL BE BURIED WITH ME...
...I DON'T KNOW WHAT TO DO WITH THEM, TBH.

I ALSO GOT CONFIRMATION
THAT ALL OTHER REMOVED ORGANS
HAD BEEN RETURNED TO THE BODY.
I GUESS I HAVE TO TAKE THEIR WORD FOR IT.
STILL...WHAT THEY DID...IT HAUNTS ME.

HOWEVER, ON THE PLUS SIDE,
IF ONE CAN CALL IT THAT,
KaRa BEING REMOVED MEANT
I WOULD AT LEAST GET TO SEE OUR BABY!
I WENT TO THE CHAPEL OF REST...
...OH WHAT A *BEAUUUTIFUL* LITTLE GIRL!

I CRADLED HER IN MY ARMS AND
NATURALLY BEGAN GENTLY ROCKING HER.
"HELLO BABEEE!"
"HEY BEAUTIFUL!"
HEAVY TEARDROPS JUST FELL OUT MY EYES
ONTO HER CLOTHES
AS I LOOKED DOWN AT HER...
...BUT I WAS *BEAMING*!

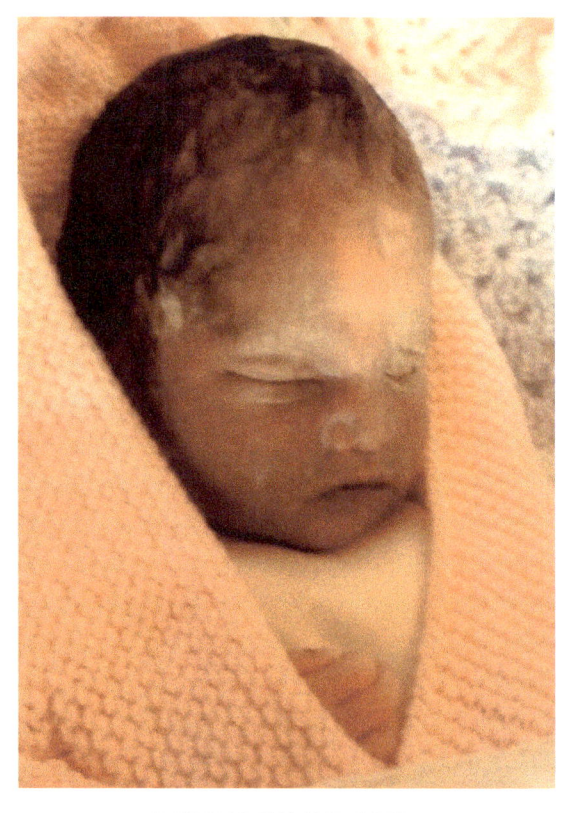

I FELT SO PROUD
TO SEE WHAT A BEAUTIFUL BABY WE'D MADE.
I WAS THRILLED!
EVEN THOUGH IT WAS SO TRAGIC,
I WAS STILL LOOKING AT MY DAUGHTER!
I'LL *NEVER* FORGET THAT DAY.
WHAT A STRANGE RANGE
OF CONFLICTING EMOTIONS.
I ASKED THAT KaRa BE RETURNED
TO KHABI'S BODY FOR BURIAL,
WHICH DULY HAPPENED.

I STILL COULDN'T BELIEVE WHAT WAS GOING ON.
I THOUGHT TO MYSELF, WHAT IF THIS ISN'T REAL,
WHAT IF KHABI'S BEEN KIDNAPPED
AND A FAKE BODY'S BEEN PUT HERE TO FOOL ME!

I ACTUALLY NEEDED
TO MAKE SURE THIS WASN'T THE CASE!
SO I REQUESTED TO SEE HER BODY AGAIN,
BUT WITH HER BODY COMPLETELY COVERED,
NOT ONLY BECAUSE I DIDN'T WANT
TO SEE HER INJURIES AGAIN,
BUT ALSO BECAUSE
I ONLY NEEDED TO SEE HER HAND.

KHABI HAD BEEN GETTING
REALLY NERVOUS ABOUT THE BIRTH
AND HAD BEEN BITING HER NAILS SO MUCH
THAT SHE'D MADE HER FINGERS BLEED.
I KNEW ANYONE FAKING THIS WOULDN'T THINK,
OR EVEN KNOW OF A DETAIL LIKE THAT...
...BUT THEY WERE INDEED BADLY BITTEN.

THIS *WAS* REAL.
WHERE DO I GO FROM HERE?
WHAT DO I DO NOW?
ALL OUR PLANS!
FINISHED!

I LITERALLY FELT GUTTED;
LIKE EVERYTHING INSIDE ME WAS GONE.
ROBBED. EMPTY. LOST. SICK. DEPRESSED.

THEN ON TOP OF ALL THE EMOTION AND FEAR,
THE FUNERAL WAS BEING DELAYED BECAUSE
THE POLICE WOULDN'T RELEASE THE BODY
UNTIL THE MAN HAD BEEN SENTENCED...
...AND THAT WAS BEING DELAYED,
WAITING FOR TWO SEPARATE DOCTORS
TO GIVE A DIAGNOSIS OF
THE SUSPECT'S MENTAL HEALTH.

THIS DELAY CAUSED SUSPICION
AMONGST SOME MEMBERS OF THE COMMUNITY,
FAMILY AND FRIENDS.
PEOPLE WERE ACCUSING ME OF LYING;
OF HIDING SOMETHING;
OF BEING A BAD HUSBAND.

PEOPLE WERE SAYING THAT SHE DIED
BECAUSE I DIDN'T WANT HER ANYMORE.
HER FRIENDS SENT ME HURTFUL MESSAGES.
TENSIONS RAN HIGH WITH HER FAMILY.
PEOPLE WERE WHISPERING,
COMING UP WITH OUTLANDISH REASONS
AS TO WHY THIS AWFUL THING HAD HAPPENED.

BUT I KNEW EVERYONE WAS HURTING...
...I KNEW THEY DIDN'T MEAN
WHAT THEY WERE SAYING.
PEOPLE WRE WERE IN SHOCK AND PAIN
AND I THINK IT SENT THEM ALL A BIT CRAZY.

KHABI JUST MEANS SO MUCH TO SO MANY!

I BUMPED INTO ONE OF
ME 'N' KHABI'S BREDRINS, BONGANI.
I EXPLAINED TO HIM THAT WE WERE STILL
WAITING FOR THE BODY TO BE RELEASED.

HIS EYES FILLED WITH WATER AS HE MUSTERED,
"YOU MEAN THE FUNERAL HASN'T HAPPENED YET!?!
YOH! MAN, *I THOUGHT I'D MISSED IT!*"

KHABI REALLY MEANT A LOT
TO A LOT OF PEOPLE.
EVERYONE WAS *DEVASTATED*.

THE COMMUNITY POURED OUT THEIR LOVE.
WHICH WAS A BEAUTIFUL THING TO SEE.

ONE NIGHT, I WAS WALKING UP TO MY FLAT,
WHEN I SAW OUR FRIEND, KIER,
WALKING TOWARDS ME OUT OF THE DARKNESS.
THEN MORE AND MORE FRIENDS APPEARED!
THEY'D BROUGHT FLOWERS AND LANTERNS.

ONE DAY, A BREDRIN OF OURS, RODDIE,
CALLED ME UP TO TELL ME HE'D MADE A TUNE,
CALLED, "RISE AND SHINE",
SUNG BY OUR FRIEND, "TEMPA",
AND THAT HE WANTED TO DEDICATE IT TO KHABI
BY PUTTING HER FACE ON THE LABEL,
WITH A DEDICATION
AND A COPY OF ONE OF KHABI'S POEMS,
"RISING PHOENIX", INCLUDED IN THE SLEEVE.

IT TOUCHED ME SO MUCH, I CRIED ON THE PHONE.
SO MANY PEOPLE DID SO MUCH...RAISING FUNDS,
MAKING FOOD, RECITING POETRY, GIVING SPEECHES.

EVEN A BEAUTIFUL ALBUM WAS PUT OUT
TO HELP RAISE FUNDS FOR THE FUNERAL COSTS;
"HIGHER LOVE" BY JAH FREE
AND VARIOUS OTHER ARTISTS, LIKE,
MALCOM "GOLDMASTER", SIS SIMIAH,
ROBEL THE "EARTHIOPIAN" AND OTHERS!
BLESS YOU ALL!

SHAUN, JIM AND MEL, KEETY, TABZ, CLIVEY, TRISH,
RODDIE, RUTHENDO, I KAYA, JAH FREE, SIMIAH,
LOVENESS, JOHNNY, MIKEY, CYPRIAN AND PATRICIA,
KIER, SALOME, TORI, SANDRA AND MANY OTHERS,
THANK YOU SO MUCH FOR ALL YOU DID.....AND DO!

KHABI WAS *SO SWEET* TO EVERYONE SHE MET.
SHE RADIATED LOVE AND CARE.
SHE HAD THE LOOK OF A REAL PRINCESS.
I'VE NEVER MET SUCH A PURE SOUL!
SO BEAUTIFUL....INSIDE *AND* OUT!

I'M SO LUCKY...I GOT TO MARRY A TRUE ANGEL!

CHAPTER 8...THE FUNERAL

EVENTUALLY, KHABI'S BODY WAS RELEASED.
THE FUNERAL WOULD BE HELD 30/08/16...
...NEARLY 4 MONTHS AFTER THE FIRE!
IT HAD BEEN AN AWFUL WAIT,
FULL OF QUESTIONS AND ANXIETY,
BUT NOW THINGS WERE FINALLY MOVING.

LIKE I SAID EARLIER,
THE COMMUNITY POURED OUT THEIR LOVE.
PEOPLE JUST KEPT COMING UP TO ME
AND TELLING ME HOW SORRY THEY WERE.
FRIENDS AND STRANGERS RAISED AND DONATED
A LOT OF MONEY FOR KHABI.

THE KINDNESS WAS OVERWHELMING.
REALLY QUITE BEAUTIFUL AND TOUCHING
TO SEE HOW MANY PEOPLE HAD BEEN AFFECTED
BY WHAT'D HAPPENED TO THE GIRL THEY
NEVER SAW ME WITHOUT.

LOCAL CHURCHES EVEN GOT INVOLVED
AND OFFERED TO DO THE SERVICE.
THEIR CONGREGATIONS
HAD DONATED MONEY
TO US TOO!

REV. MOON, REV. ANDREW
AND YOUR CONGREGATIONS,
BLESS YOU! THANK YOU ALL SO MUCH!

THIS ALL MEANT I COULD GET SOME FAMILY
OVER FROM SOUTH AFRICA FOR THE FUNERAL.
IT ALSO ENABLED ME TO GET
A HORSE DRAWN CARRIAGE
TO TRANSPORT THE COFFIN,
AS KHABI LOVED THEM, SAYING,
"HORSES ARE LIKE THE SUPERMODELS
OF THE ANIMAL KINGDOM!"
WHEN WE WENT HORSE RIDING IN SWAZILAND.

THE COFFIN
WAS A BEAUTIFUL WILLOW BASKET.

I'D BEEN USING THE INTERNET AT THE LIBRARY
TO SEARCH FOR THE NICEST ONE I COULD FIND.
THAT, IN ITSELF, WAS A HORRIBLE EXPERIENCE,
COFFIN SHOPPIN'...
...FOR MY *WIFE!*

TIME FOR TEARS AGAIN.
I WAS HOLDING IT DOWN,
BUT THE TEARS WERE UNSTOPPABLE.
SCHOOL KIDS WERE THERE, TALKING ABOUT ME.
ANYWAY I WENT THROUGH THEM ALL.
I WANTED SOMETHING NATURAL AND BEAUTIFUL
AND WHEN I FOUND THE WILLOW ONE,
THE SEARCH WAS OVER....KHABI LOVES TREES,
HUGGING THEM LIKE LONG LOST RELATIVES
WHENEVER SHE COULD.
PLUS I HAD A WILLOW TREE IN MY GARDEN
WHERE I GREW UP.

I GOT EVERYTHING SORTED.
BOOKED FLIGHTS, SORTED ACCOMODATION,
GOT EMERGENCY VISAS,
SORTED OUT FOOD FOR THE WAKE
GOT THE ORDERS OF SERVICE DONE,
GOT THE MUSIC SORTED.
I WAS SHOCKED I'D GOT IT ALL DONE
'COS I'M USUALLY SO BADLY ORGANIZED.

KHABI'S MUM AND BIOLOGICAL FATHER, NONKY AND SAM
(WHO HAD NOT SEEN EACH OTHER FOR MANY YEARS)
AND OUR BROTHER, LEFA, FLEW FROM JO'BURG,
WHILE A GOOD FRIEND OF OURS, KARIN,
HITCH-HIKED FROM KNYSNA TO CAPE TOWN
AND FLEW FROM THERE.
THIS WAS ALL NOTHING SHORT OF A MIRACLE...
...ONE THAT ONLY KHABI COULD PULL OFF!

YOU SEE, FOR BLACK PEOPLE TO BE GRANTED
A VISA APPLICATION IN SOUTH AFRICA IS
USUALLY SUCH A LONG PROCESS OF
BEING DENIED, APPLYING AGAIN, BEING DENIED,
APPLYING AGAIN, EACH TIME PAYING MONEY,
ON TOP OF TRAVEL MONEY
TO AND FROM THE VISA OFFICE, WHICH IS
LOCATED MANY, MANY MILES FROM ANYONE!
SO BLACK PEOPLE'S MOVEMENTS
ARE STILL BEING LIMITED IN SOUTH AFRICA,
EVEN DOWN TO THE ROAD LAY-OUTS AND CAREFUL
POSITIONING OF TOWNSHIPS AND SUBURBS,
BUT THAT'S A WHOLE OTHER STORY TO BE TOLD.

TRAVELLING FROM SA TO THE UK WAS,
FOR EVERYONE, A BITTER-SWEET EXPERIENCE,
AS, WHILE IT WAS THEIR PRECIOUS HEART'S FUNERAL,
IT WAS STILL AN EXCITING EXPERIENCE,
FILLED WITH JOY TO SEE ONE ANOTHER
AFTER SAYING GOODBYE, 3 YEARS EARLIER.

KARIN, OUR RASTAFARI SISTA ARRIVED FIRST.
SHE WAS BUZZING WITH NERVOUS EXCITEMENT
WHEN I MET HER AT HEATHROW AIRPORT.
SHE SAID SHE HAD BEEN SO NERVOUS,
TRAVELLING AROUND 20 HOURS ON HER OWN!

THAT'S THE LENGTH SOME WOULD GO TO BE HERE
FOR KHABI; THAT'S HOW SPECIAL SHE WAS...*IS*.
EVEN AN OLD LADY WE DIDN'T KNOW
TURNED UP AT THE FUNERAL,
FROM MILES AWAY,
JUST BECAUSE SHE'D SEEN KHABI IN TOWN
AND MUST'VE SEEN HER SMILE
OR FELT HER SPIRIT RADIATING SUNSHINE
AND WAS SO SADDENED
TO HEAR WHAT'D HAPPENED TO HER.

I WAS FEELING SO WEAK IN THOSE DAYS
THE JOURNEY TO THE AIRPORT ON THE TRAIN
FILLED ME WITH FEAR AND ANXIETY:
WHAT IF I FAINT? WHAT IF I CRY?
WHAT IF I'M SICK? I CAN'T DO IT!
THIS WAS MADE WORSE BY THE FACT THAT I
WOULD HAVE TO BE TRAVELLING IN THE MORNING,

WHICH WAS WHEN I WOULD EXPERIENCE
THE WORST EFFECTS OF THE SHOCK;
THE NAUSEA, CHEST BANGING AND FAINTNESS.

THANKFULLY, OUR RASTA BROTHER, CLIVEY,
DROVE ME THERE TO COLLECT SISTA KARIN.
IRIE, LOVEGROVE!

IT WAS THE SAME WHEN I HAD TO COLLECT
SAM, NONKY AND LEFA,
BUT I WAS EVEN MORE STRESSED THIS TIME, AS
LEFA AND NONKY WERE LANDING AT HEATHROW,
BUT SAM WAS LANDING MOMENTS LATER
AT GATWICK, SO IT WAS GONNA BE A MAD DASH,
'COS I DIDN'T WANNA KEEP HIM WAITING THERE.

THANKFULLY, YET AGAIN,
ONE OF OUR REGGAE FAMILY, RICHARD,
WAS RUNNING ME ABOUT,
SAVING ME A WHOLE HEAP OF STRESS AND ENERGY.
PEACE, MAN!

UNFORTUNATELY, FOR ONE REASON AND ANOTHER,
MY AUNTY, TWO UNCLES AND THREE COUSINS
COULDN'T GET FROM NORFOLK AND KENT
TO THE FUNERAL
IN ESSEX.

THIS *REALLY* SADDENED ME, 'COS
I MISSED THEM AND WANTED/NEEDED
TO SEE THEM SO MUCH.

I HADN'T SEEN THEM FOR ABOUT 7 OR 8 YEARS,
SINCE KHABI AND I WENT TO NORFOLK WITH MUM
TO VISIT THEM. THAT WAS SUCH A LOVELY TIME.
IT WAS THE FIRST TIME I'D SEEN THEM
SINCE MY DAD DIED 2 YEARS PRIOR.
I'M SO GLAD WE WENT, OTHERWISE
THEY'D'VE NEVER MET KHABI!
AS FOR MY DAD'S SIDE OF THE FAMILY...
...I BUMPED INTO MY UNCLE SOME TIME
AFTER RETURNING FROM AFRICA.
IN THE RUSH, I HADN'T TOLD HIM
WE WERE GOING AND, SOON AFTER
REACHING AFRICA, I LOST MY PHONE ON THE BUS
AND MUM DIDN'T HAVE HIS NUMBER,
SO WHEN I SAW HIM IN THE STREET,
I WAS SO PLEASED TO SEE HIM!
YET....THIS WAS WHAT WAS SAID:

"YOU'RE BACK THEN!"

"YEAH!"

"I DIDN'T KNOW YOU'D GONE!"

"I KNOW, I'M SO SORRY,
I LOST MY PHONE WHEN I GOT THERE!
LET ME TAKE YOUR NUMBER AGAIN!"

"ERR, NO!
I'D RATHER LEAVE IT LIKE IT IS, I THINK!"
I NEVER SAW HIM AGAIN. HE'S DEAD NOW.

IT WAS ALL SO SURREAL,
HAVING SAM, LEFA AND NONKY,
FROM RANDFONTEIN, SAT IN THE CAR,
FLOATING ABOUT IN *SOUTHEND-ON-SEA!*
PLUS, IT WAS STRANGE, MONUMENTAL EVEN,
SEEING SAM AND NONKY TOGETHER,
AS THEY HADN'T SEEN EACH OTHER IN DECADES.

BEFORE LONG, THEY WANTED TO GO AND SEE
KHABI'S BODY BEFORE THE FUNERAL.
I *BEGGED* THEM NOT TO.
I *REALLY* DIDN'T WANT THEM TO SEE
THEIR BELOVED "KHANO" IN SUCH A BAD STATE.
BUT THEY NEEDED TO SEE WHAT HAD HAPPENED.
THEY NEEDED TO SEE IT WAS REAL,
LIKE I DID, THEY NEEDED CLOSURE AND
THEY NEEDED TO SEE HER ONE MORE TIME.

HER PARENTS SEEMED TO COPE WELL.
BROTHER LEFA WAS SHELL-SHOCKED.
HIS EXPRESSION WAS JUST LOST AND DAZED.
HE DID'T SAY MUCH AS WE DROVE BACK TO MUM'S.

I HATED ALL OF THIS.
NONE OF IT SHOULD'VE BEEN HAPPENING.
I FELT LIKE I'D LET *THEM* DOWN
AS WELL AS KHABI AND KaRa.
LIKE I FAILED TO KEEP THEIR TREASURE SAFE.
WITH SHAME IN MY HEART AND
REGRET AND SORROW IN MY VOICE, I TOLD THEM,
"I'M SORRY SHE WASN'T SAFE IN MY HOME."

KHABI'S PARENTS HAD SEPARATED
WHEN KHABI AND LEFA WERE VERY YOUNG,
SO SAM NEEDED SOMEWHERE TO STAY
SEPARATELY FROM THE OTHERS,
WHO WERE SPENDING SOME TIME AT A B'N'B
AND SOME TIME WITH LOCAL
SOUTH AFRICAN FRIENDS OF OURS, SO
SAM CAME TO SLEEP ON THE COUCH AT MINE...
...WITH ALL THE SOOT ON THE WALLS STILL!

I MEAN MY BLESSED FRIENDS, SOLOMON,
JASON AND HIS WIFE, ANNIE,
HAD COME DOWN FROM LONDON, BLESS 'EM,
ARMED WITH SPONGES, DETTOL, BUCKETS,
STEAM-CLEANERS AND BRANDY
AND CLEANED THE PLACE UP FOR ME,
BUT IT WAS STILL PRETTY GRIM,
SLEEPING IN THAT COLD, EMPTY BED,
STARING AT THE MARKS ON THE WALL
PICTURING THE FEAR AND PANIC
KHABI MUST HAVE FELT THAT NIGHT.

THE NEXT MORNING, I WAS AWAKE EARLY,
GOING INTO SHOCK AS PER USUAL,
HEAVING INTO A BAG. IT WOKE SAM UP.
HIS FACE! HE WAS SO WORRIED ABOUT ME.
FINALLY, THE FUNERAL WAS UPON US.
THE NIGHT BEFORE,
MY FRIEND, JIM, CAME TO SEE HOW I WAS...
...A BAG OF NERVES, TALKING FAST
AND IN A KIND OF DAZE.

I WAS REALLY GRATEFUL FOR THE VISIT.
I NEEDED TO LAUGH.
I NEEDED NOT TO THINK ABOUT
WHAT THE NEXT DAY WAS.

YES JAH LION! YOU'VE BEEN A STAR!
DRIVING ME TO LONDON
FOR THE HEARING. FEEDING ME UP.
GETTING ME AWAY FROM IT ALL.
BLESS YOU AND MEL AND D!

FINALLY, KHABI'S FUNERAL DAY ARRIVED
AND IT WAS A TRULY BEAUTIFUL DAY...
...THE SUN BATHED US ALL IN GOLDEN LIGHT,
AS IF WE WERE IN KHABI'S PRESENCE ONCE MORE!

I KNOW LIFE IS ETERNAL.
I KNOW ONLY THE BODY DIES.
I KNEW IT WAS ALL AN ILLUSION
OF THE PHYSICAL PERSPECTIVE, BUT
I STILL COULDN'T BELIEVE WHAT WAS GOING ON,
WHAT I WAS WITNESSING/BEING PART OF.

I CAN'T BELIEVE THIS IS WHAT HAPPENED
TO HER IN THIS LIFE. OF ALL PEOPLE...
...YOU WOULDN'T WANT *ANYTHING* BAD
TO HAPPEN TO THIS *WONDERFUL, SWEET* GIRL.
A TRUE CHRISTIAN. CHRIST-LIKE. *CHRISTINE!*
HONESTLY, WHEN THE DAY OF JUDGEMENT COMES,
I WOULDN'T BE SUPRISED TO SEE KHABI DESCENDING,
WITH A HOST OF ANGELS FROM ON HIGH!

THAT'S HOW PURE A SPIRIT SHE IS
AND HOW UPRIGHT SHE LIVED.

THE FUNERAL WENT QUITE SMOOTHLY.
BUT IT ALL FELT SO WRONG.
A FUNERAL FOR KHABI! *AND KaRa!*
THE LID OF THE COFFIN COULD HARDLY CLOSE,
AS KHABI WAS SO HEAVILY PREGNANT.
IT WAS ALL DOING MY HEAD AND MY HEART IN.
I WAS FOCUSED ON ONE THING, THOUGH...
...BLESS THEM BEFORE THEY GO INTO THE EARTH.

BESING A RASTAFARIAN,
I HAD MY ETHIOPIAN CROSS, MY MESKEL,
THAT MY DAD HAD GIFTED ME WITH, YEARS AGO.
I WANTED TO BLESS THEM IN AMHARIC (ETHIOPIC).

AFTER THE SERVICE I CHOSE MY MOMENT:
"SELASSEWOCH ANDEM SOSTEM NACHEW"
("THE TRINITY IS ONE AND THREE")
"BE SEME AB, WE WOLD, WE MENFES Q'IDDUS...
...**AHAD** AMLAK!"
(IN THE NAME OF THE FATHER,
THE SON, THE HOLY SPIRIT...
...**ONE** GOD!")

THEN ME AND ALL "THE MAN DEM"
TOOK TURNS FILLING IN THE GRAVE...
...THE LAST THING WE COULD DO FOR HER.

SUDDENLY THERE WAS SINGING!

A LOVELY FRIEND OF OURS, THAPELO,
BROKE OUT INTO A BEAUTIFUL AFRICAN SONG.
DAD, SAM ALSO PIPED UP.
IT WAS ALL VERY MOVING.

THEN THERE WAS A MOMENT
WHERE I JUST FOUND MYSELF ALONE
JUST STANDING LOOKING AT THEIR GRAVE
NOT KNOWING WHAT TO SAY OR DO NEXT.

I WAS LOST. ON SO MANY LEVELS...JUST LOST.
I STILL AM TO BE HONEST.

I LOOKED AROUND AND SAW MY MUM
STANDING A LITTLE DISTANCE FROM ME,
LOOKING EXACTLY HOW I FELT...
...ALONE, LOST AND CONFUSED.

I WANTED TO GO HUG HER...BUT I WAS FROZEN.
I COULDN'T MOVE...OR EVEN SPEAK.

THANKFULLY MY BREDRIN JASON'S QUEEN, ANNIE,
SPOTTED MUM AND WENT TO HER.

I THINK JASON MUST'VE POURED ME A
CHRIS BLACKWELL RUM...OR FOUR!
IT WAS A HOT, SUNNY DAY,
I WAS IN A BLACK SUIT,
I HADN'T EATEN ALL MOURNING
AND I DON'T USUALLY DRINK.
I'M AFRAID, I WAS VERY, *VERY* DRUNK!

NEXT MINUTE,
I WAS RAMBLING LOUDLY IN THE LIMOUSINE.
STILL, I FELT MUCH BETTER THAN BEFORE!!!

THE SUN GRADUALLY GOT MORE AND MORE GOLDEN.
THERE WAS A MAGICAL BEAUTY TO THAT DAY.
KHABI'S RADIANCE WAS SHINING DOWN ON US.

FABIAN ("Fabes")
NICKI   *TIZIAH*

SOLOMON   *JASON*   *SHAUN*
("Solo")   *("Price")*   *("Dread")*
"THE MAN DEM"

THAT EVENING,
WE ALL PLAYED TUNES FOR KHABI
DOWN THE BOROUGH HOTEL PUB...
...THE VENUE I WAS AT THE NIGHT OF THE FIRE.
KHABI AND I USED TO DJ REGGAE MUSIC.
MY DJ NAME IS, JAH LOVE. KHABI WAS, JAH LIGHT.

HERE WE ARE DJ-ING ON THE BEACH.

SO I PLAYED KHABI'S TUNES:
A JAH LIGHT SELECTION!
THEN IT WAS DONE.
THE WORST THING I'D EVER HAD TO DO WAS OVER.
THE DAY I'D BEEN STRESSING ABOUT
AND DREADING THE MOST
HAD PASSED.
WHAT A RELIEF!

IN THE DAYS AFTER THE FUNERAL, MUM AND I
TRIED TO MAKE THE MOST OF OUR TIME
WITH THE FAMILY, BEFORE THEY WENT BACK TO SA,
BUT WE WERE ALL FRAZZLED.

THE EMOTIONS, THE STRESS, THE SHOCK!
IT TOOK ITS TOLL ON US ALL.

KHABI'S DAD, SAM

WE DID DO SOME TOURISTY THINGS;
WE VISITED LONDON, GOT FISH 'N' CHIPS,
WENT TO THE SEASIDE, GOT MORE FISH 'N' CHIPS,
THEY WERE HOOKED, AS IT WERE, LOL!
WE TOOK THEM TO THE PLACES KHABI LOVES
AND PLACES OF MY CHILDHOOD.
THEN, ALL TOO SUDDENLY, THEY WERE GONE AGAIN.
THEIR ABSENCE IS STILL PALPABLE.
WE MISS THE WHOLE FAMILY *TERRIBLY.*

SOME TIME DURING THE WEEKS THAT FOLLOWED,
I FOUND KHABI HAD BEEN
COMPILING THE POETRY SHE'D BEEN WRITING
OVER THE YEARS.
RATHER POIGNANTLY,
KHABI HAD TITLED HER POETRY,
"SPIRIT WORDZ"!!!

FURTHERMORE,
SHE'D WRITTEN A POEM CALLED,
"RISING PHOENIX",
WHERE SHE TALKS ABOUT
PASSING THROUGH THE DOOR OF TRUTH
AND HER SOUL SURVIVING THE FLAMES!
IT REALLY SEEMS LIKE SHE KNEW
WHAT WAS COMING…
…AND THAT HER SOUL WOULD SURVIVE!

I SET ABOUT ORGANISING THE POETRY
ACCORDING TO THE CONTENTS PAGE
SHE HAD ALREADY TYPED OUT.
SHE'D ALSO GATHERED
SOME PICTURES TOGETHER,
SO I JUST PAIRED THEM UP WITH THE POEMS
THAT SEEMED TO REFERENCE THEM.

IT WAS EMOTIONAL TO SAY THE LEAST,
BUT IT WAS SOMETHING POSITIVE TO DO
AND I WANTED TO HONOUR KHABI'S WISHES.
MOST OF ALL, THOUGH,
I WANTED HER SWEET, GENTLE VOICE TO BE HEARD.

I PUT ALL MY ENERGY INTO COMPLETING HER BOOK
AND UPDATING MY BOOK.

IT REALLY KEPT ME GOING.
IT DIDN'T TAKE MY MIND OFF OF THINGS THOUGH,
BECAUSE I WAS DOCUMENTING
DETAILS OF WHAT HAD HAPPENED.

PLUS I WAS GOING THROUGH OUR PHOTOS
TO FIND IMAGES FOR THE COVER
AND FOR THE BOOK, BECAUSE
I REALLY WANTED TO CONVEY KHABI'S SPIRIT
TO THE READER, SO THEY MIGHT FEEL
AS IF THEY HAD MET HER AND
WITNESSED/FELT HER WARM RADIANCE.

SO IT WAS REALLY TOUGH GOING,
BUT WELL WORTH IT.

"SPIRIT WORDZ",
BY
BOKHABINYANA RADIANCE LOVELIGHT
IS AVAILABLE NOW!

WATERSTONES AND OTHER LOCAL SHOPS,
LIKE, "JOHNNIES NUMBER ONE CARIBBEAN FOOD",
"SOUTH" AND "OH YEAH!" HAVE BEEN KINDLY
SUPPORTING AND STOCKING OUR BOOKS.
BLESSINGS TO THEM ALL!

THEN CAME THE NEXT TRIAL....*THE TRIAL!*

CHAPTER 9...THE TRIAL, BY FIRE

THE SENTENCING OF THE SUSPECT,
LILLO TROISI,
AN ITALIAN MAN FROM LONDON,
WAS THE NEXT ORDEAL.
I'D NEVER MET HIM OR SEEN HIS FACE,
OTHER THAN SEEING THE IMAGE BELOW
IN THE LOCAL NEWSPAPER, AFTER THE EVENT.

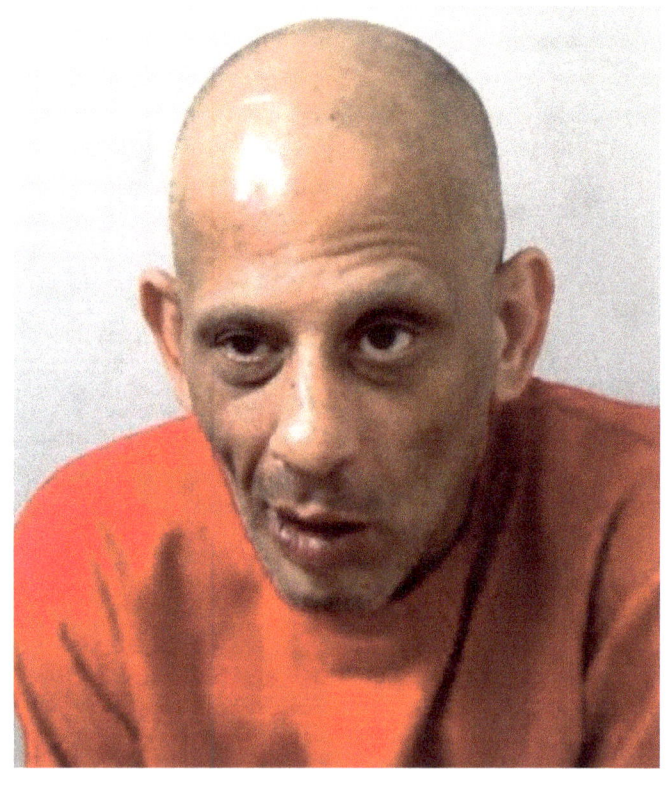

I HAVE STUDIED THIS FACE.

THIS FACE SAYS:
"OH NO!"
"WHAT'VE I DONE!?!"
"I'M SORRY!"
THIS PERSON
SEEMS TROUBLED
AND CONFUSED.

THIS FACE SAYS:
"YEAH I DID IT!"
"SO WHAT!!!???"
"I DON'T CARE!"
THIS PERSON
SEEMS AMUSED
AND CALCULATING.

TWO TOTALLY DIFFERENT PEOPLE...IN ONE MAN.
ALMOST PHYSIO-SCHIZOPHRENIC.

I KEEP VISUALISING HIM COMING UP THE STAIRS,
DOING WHAT HE DID BEHIND MY BACK,
THEN CREEPING BACK DOWN AGAIN,
ESPECIALLY WHEN THE LIFT IS BROKEN
AND I HAVE TO USE THE STAIRS,
IT'S A REAL, LIVING NIGHTMARE.

I WONDERED WHAT I WOULD DO
WHEN I CAME FACE TO FACE
WITH THE MAN WHO TOOK MY FAMILY FROM ME...
...WOULD I SHOUT AT HIM?
WOULD I CRY?
WOULD I VOMIT?
WOULD I FREEZE?
WOULD I LUNGE AT HIS THROAT?

WHEN I FINALLY DID SEE HIM IN COURT...
...I WAS SHOCKED AT WHAT I SAW...AND FELT!
THE MAN IN THE DOCK
LOOKED *TOTALLY DIFFERENT*
FROM THE MAN IN THE PICTURE!

NOW HE HAD HAIR
AND HAD PUT A LOT OF WEIGHT ON,
BECAUSE HE WAS NOW *FINALLY BEING GIVEN*
THE MEDICATION AND CARE HE, FOR MANY REASONS
THAT I WILL BRIEFLY TOUCH UPON AS WE PROGRESS,
HAD NOT BEEN ABLE TO GET FOR AROUND 16 MONTHS!

HE HARDLY LOOKED MY WAY ONCE.
MY SIGHT WAS FIXED ON HIM.
WAS THIS REALLY THE GUY!?!
I STUDIED HIM AS MUCH AS I STUDIED HIS PICTURE.
HE LOOKED LIKE HE DIDN'T KNOW
WHAT THE HELL WAS GOING ON.
YOU COULD SEE HE WAS NOW DRUGGED UP.
HE REMINDED ME OF SOME OF MY OLD CLIENTS;
DOPEY; ALMOST DRIBBLING; TRANQUIL-IZED.

HE LOOKED ABSOLUTELY LOST.
TO BE HONEST...
...IT WAS A VERY SAD SIGHT AND
I CAN'T BELIEVE HOW SAD I FELT LOOKING AT HIM.
SUCH CONFLICTING EMOTIONS I WAS HAVING.

AS I LEARNED MORE ABOUT HIS ILLNESS
AND THE FACTS AROUND HIS BREAKDOWN,
SUCH AS HIS BECOMING SO UNWELL
AS TO BE SO DISTURBED
BY THE SOUNDS OF THE WORLD
AND THE VOICES IN HIS HEAD THAT
HE HAD TO SPEND TIME SITTING IN FIELDS...
...WELL...IT MADE ME WANT TO CRY!!!???

AS I STUDIED THIS MAN BEFORE ME,
I COULD SEE THAT *THIS PERSON*
WAS PHYSICALLY AND MENTALLY
NOT THE PERSON WHO SET THE FIRE!
ONE CAN'T IMAGINE THE TORTURE
OF FINDING OUT WHAT HE'D DONE,
WHEN HE BECAME CLEARER MINDED
UPON RE-UPTAKE OF MEDICATION!

LILLO HAS BEEN ILL MOST OF HIS LIFE.
HE BEGAN TO EXPERIENCE MENTAL ILL-HEALTH
AROUND THE TIME HE BURNED HIS SCHOOL DOWN,
WITH HIS FRIEND, AGED JUST 12!

THIS DOES MAKE ME WONDER, THOUGH...

...WAS LILLO JUST PURELY
A BADLY BEHAVED PERSON;
WAS HE BORN WITH MENTAL HEALTH ISSUES...OR
DID <u>*HIS FRIEND** ENCOURAGE HIM TO SET THAT FIRE,
WHICH TRAUMATISED LILLO AND CAUSED
HIS MENTAL ILL HEALTH!!!???</u>
FOR ME, THIS REMAINS TO BE SEEN.

**HE'D BEEN SECTIONED
TO A SECURE MENTAL HEALTH UNIT *SEVERAL* TIMES,**
WHERE HE WOULD RECEIVE MEDICATION
AND BECOME WELL**...HOWEVER...**
...HE KEPT GETTING RELEASED,
THEN HE'D DEFAULT ON HIS MEDICATION
AND BECOME UNWELL AGAIN.
**<u>THIS IS THE CYCLE
THAT NEEDS TO BE BROKEN.</u>**

AT SOME POINT,
IT MUST BE ADMITTED
THAT LILLO IS NOT WELL ENOUGH
TO BE LEFT TO HIS OWN DEVICES.
*IT MUST ALSO BE ADMITTED
THAT <u>HE HAS LOST THE RIGHT</u>
TO BE LEFT TO HIS OWN DEVICES.*

I JUST DON'T THINK IT'S SAFE ENOUGH *OR FAIR ENOUGH*
**- <u>NOR IS HE INNOCENT ENOUGH</u> -
FOR HIM TO BE TRUSTED OR *PRIVILEGED*
WITH TIME ALONE.**

*Where is that friend now? Is he safe/well/being looked after/monitored?

FOR MANY YEARS,
**LILLO'S MENTAL HEALTH HAD BEEN MANAGED
BY GIVING HIM A DEPOT INJECTION,
WHICH IS WHERE AN ANTI-PSYCHOTIC DRUG IS
ADMINISTERED MONTHLY BY TRAINED STAFF,**
WHERE HIS MEDICATION COMPLIANCE
COULD BE MONITORED AND RECORDED,
RESPONDING EFFECTIVELY TO ANY FLUCTUATION.

**HOWEVER, WHEN HE MOVED
TO MY AREA (ESSEX) FROM LONDON,
HE –** *AND HIS GP!!!???* **– WERE UNABLE
TO SOURCE THIS DEPOT INJECTION!
WHY WAS IT LEFT TO** *HIM* **TO DO!!!???**

IS IT NOT KNOWN
THAT MANY PATIENTS
DON'T WANT THEIR MEDICATION
AND WOULD USE MOVING HOME
AS AN OPPORTUNITY TO DEFAULT ON MEDICATION!?!
SURELY SOMETHING SO STRESSFULL AS MOVING HOME,
ESPECIALLY OVER SUCH A LARGE DISTANCE,
SHOULD BE CAUSE FOR EXTRA SUPPORT!?!

AS THINGS STOOD...HE COULDN'T STAY WELL.
WE COULD HEAR HIM GRADUALLY DESCENDING
DEEPER AND DEEPER INTO DESPAIR,
AS HE HAD BEGUN TO MAKE
TERRIBLE SCREACHING SOUNDS,
ALMOST LIKE HE WAS BEING TORTURED.

HIS FAMILY
HAD BECOME *VERY CONCERNED* ABOUT HIM
AND DID <u>EVERYTHING</u> THEY COULD
TO GET THEIR LOVED ONE
THE HELP HE NEEDED/*WANTED*,
BUT NO ONE SEEMED TO BE RESPONDING
THE WAY THEY HAD HOPED,
AS THEY WERE SENT ROUND IN CIRCLES,
FROM ONE INSTITUTION BACK TO THE OTHER.

SURELY FAMILY INPUT SHOULD BE CRUCIAL
AND PROMPTLY RESPONDED TO
WHEN DEALING WITH A PERSON
WITH MENTAL HEALTH,
AS THEY HAVE THE MOST INTIMATE KNOWLEDGE
OF THEIR RELATIVES BEHAVIOURS,
TRIGGERS AND WARNING SIGNS!?!

WE DID WHAT *WE* COULD TO GET INTERVENTION,
BUT NOTHING APPEARED TO HAPPEN
OR CHANGE AS A RESULT.

CLEARLY THERE IS A SERIOUS FLAW HERE,
WHEN SO MANY PEOPLE
ARE CONCERNED ABOUT A PERSON,
BUT NONE OF THEM ARE ABLE
GET THE RESPONSE NEEDED!

***EVEN LILLO TOOK HIMSELF
TO A MENTAL HEALTH UNIT...
...WHERE HE WAS APPARENTLY TURNED AWAY,
AS HE WAS KNOWN AS A TROUBLE-MAKER!!!***

SO LILLO DID WHAT HE DID AS A RESULT OF
NOT RECEIVING HIS MEDICATION
FOR OVER A YEAR AND A HALF.

HE WAS ARRESTED
TWO DAYS AFTER SETTING THE FIRE;
THE DAY WE WERE BOOKED IN
FOR OUR FIRST PRE-NATAL CLASS;
THE DAY WE *SHOULD'VE* CELEBRATED
8 YEARS TOGETHER, BUT WAS, INSTEAD,
THE DAY KHABI WAS PRONOUNCED DEAD.

HOWEVER, THE ARREST WAS FOR ANOTHER INCIDENT,
SO HE WAS PASSED OUT OF POLICE HANDS TO THE
CRIMINAL JUSTICE LIASON AND DIVERSIONS TEAM,
WHO ASSESSED HIS MENTAL STATE
AND *FOUND NO SIGN OF PSYCHOSIS
OR NEGATIVE INTENT IN HIM...AND LET HIM GO...*
...UNAWARE HE WAS THE ONE WHO SET THE FIRE
THAT KILLED MY WIFE AND CHILD,
EVEN THOUGH HE'D BEEN CONVICTED OF ARSON *AND
LIVED IN THE FLAT BELOW THEIR LATEST ARSON VICTIMS!*

WHEN I BROUGHT THIS UP WITH THE POLICE,
THEY TOLD ME THAT *THEY DO NOT HAVE ACCESS
TO INFORMATION ABOUT PEOPLE'S MENTAL HEALTH
OR HISTORICAL CRIMES.*
**THIS IS IN SPITE OF OVER A HUNDRED FAMILES
LOSING SOMEONE AT THE HANDS OF SOMEONE
WITH SEVERE MENTAL HEALTH ISSUES EACH YEAR.**
IT'S QUITE RIGHT THAT THAT INFORMATION
SHOULD BE PRIVATE AND CONFIDENTIAL, *BUT...*

...WHEN THEIR HISTORY IMPLIES
A POTENTIAL RISK TO THEMSELVES
OR TO THE PUBLIC, *THIS INFORMATION
SHOULD THEN BE READILY AVAILABLE
TO INVESTIGATING OFFICERS*,
SHOULD IT NOT!?!

THIS WOULD GIVE THEM A BETTER SENSE
OF THE RISK AND URGENCY OF A SITUATION,
ALSO GIVING THEM A BETTER UNDERSTANDING
OF HOW BEST TO MANAGE/RESPOND TO THEM,
REDUCING THE RISK TO THEMSELVES AND OTHERS.

BUT WHEN I POINTED THIS OUT,
I WAS AGREED WITH, FOLLOWED BY BEING TOLD
THEY COULDN'T DO ANYTHING ABOUT IT!!!???

TWO DAYS AFTER BEING LET GO,
LILLO WAS RE-ARRESTED FOR THE FIRE,
ON THE 11TH OF MAY...THEY DAY OF OUR
SIXTH WEDDING ANNIVERSARY.

VERY FORTUNATELY,
THE TRIAL WAS NOT A LENGTHY PROCESS
AS LILLO ADMITTED TO SETTING THE FIRE,
PLEADING MANSLAUGHTER
RATHER THAN MURDER,
AS HE SAID
HE DIDN'T THINK ANYONE
WOULD GET HURT!

HIS ACTIONS WERE BLAMED ON EXTREME PSYCHOSIS.

THE TRIAL HAD BEEN DELAYED
TO THE FOLLOWING YEAR,
DUE TO THE JUDGE REQUIRING CONFORMATION
OF LILLO'S MENTAL STATE
FROM TWO SEPARATE PROFESSIONALS.

NO ONE SEEMED TO WANT TO BE THE ONE WHO
EITHER CONFIRMED OR DENIED HOW ILL HE WAS!
ULTIMATELY, TWO WERE FOUND WHO CONFIRMED
LILLO WAS INDEED *EXTREMELY* ILL
AT THE TIME OF THE INCIDENT.

**LILLO HAD BEEN ARRESTED FOR
ARSON, BEING WRECKLESS AS TO ENDANGER LIFE
AND CHILD DESTRUCTION.**

THE JUDGE TOLD LILLO
THAT HAD HE NOT BEEN SO VERY ILL,
SHE WOULD HAVE SENTENCED HIM TO LIFE.
**INSTEAD HE WAS CHARGED WITH ARSON AND
MANSLAUGHTER, AS SHE SAID THE ACT OF ARSON
"SUBSUMED" THE OTHER CHARGES(!!???).**

SO LILLO WAS PLACED, INDEFINITELY,
IN A SECURE MENTAL HEALTH UNIT
WITH CERTAIN CONDITIONS,
MEANING THE MINISTRY OF JUSTICE
WOULD HAVE THE FINAL SAY
IF/WHEN LILLO WOULD APPEAL
TO RETURN TO LIVING IN THE COMMUNITY.

THE SENTENCING WAS HELD
AT THE OLD BAILEY, IN LONDON.
WHEN IT WAS FINISHED, WE CAME OUTSIDE
ONLY TO BE GREETED BY A CROWD OF PRESS.

MY FAMILY LIASON OFFICER HAD WARNED ME
THAT THEY WOULD BE WAITING,
SO I COULD HAVE A CHANCE TO
PREPARE MYSELF.

I THINK I SAID SOMETHING LIKE,
"IT'S REALLY SAD! NONE OF THIS HAD TO HAPPEN.
YOU KNOW, I UNDERSTAND MENTAL HEALTH
AND THAT HE WAS LET DOWN...WE ALL WERE.
THIS HAPPENED BECAUSE
THERE'S NOT ENOUGH LOVE IN THE SYSTEM;
THERE'S NOT ENOUGH CARE IN CARE."

THE POLICE THEN SUGGESTED
WE GO FOR SOME COFFEE, SO WE FOUND A PLACE
AND SAT DOWN AND THEY ALL GOT THEIR CAFFEINE
NEEDS MET. I HAD A JUICE.

I WANTED TO KNOW MORE ABOUT
WHAT'D JUST HAPPENED IN THERE;
WHAT WAS SAID...WHAT DID IT ALL MEAN.
I WAS ASSURED BY THE POLICE
THAT LILLO WOULD PROBABLY SPEND
A GOOD TEN YEARS IN THE UNIT
BEFORE BEING CONSIDERED FOR RELEASE,
BECOMING AN OLD MAN IN THERE.

I ASKED THEM WHETHER, IF HE WAS EVER RELEASED,
HE WOULD HAVE STAFF WITH HIM CONSTANTLY.
THEY CONFIRMED THIS WOULD LIKELY BE THE CASE.
I WAS GLAD TO HEAR THAT AND REMINDED THEM,
I NEVER WANTED LILLO TO GO TO PRISON FOR THIS,
BECAUSE I UNDERSTOOD HIS MENTAL HEALTH,
BUT... I DID WANT HIM TO LOSE HIS FREEDOM
BY BEING ESCORTED EVERYWHERE,
JUST LIKE *MY* CLIENTS WERE.

EVERYBODY DRANK UP AND THAT WAS THAT.
CASE CLOSED. EVERYONE DISPERSED,
BUT I STILL HAD SO MANY QUESTIONS
THAT THEY COULD NOT ANSWER.
IT FELT LIKE EVERYONE WAS HAPPY TO LET LILLO
BE THE "FALL GUY" AND TAKE ALL THE BLAME,
BUT I FELT LIKE THIS WASN'T FAIR.
I WANTED TO KNOW HOW SOMETHING LIKE THIS
COULD HAPPEN IN A SYSTEM
THAT SHOULD BE WELL EXPERIENCED EOUGH
AND WELL EQUIPPED ENOUGH
TO PREDICT AND PREVENT SUCH INCIDENTS.

SO I STARTED ASKING THE QUESTIONS I HAD.
MY SEARCH FOR ANSWERS CULMINATED
IN AN INTERNAL POLICE INVESTIGATION,
AN EXTERNAL INVESTIGATION INTO THE
MENTAL HEALTH SERVICES IN ESSEX
AND THE RE-OPENING OF THE INQUEST,
WHICH IS APPARENTLY UNHEARD OF
AS IT IMPLIES THAT SOMETHING WAS MISSED
DURING THE ORIGINAL INQUEST!

DUE TO THE TIME NEEDED
TO GET ALL THE RIGHT INTERESTED PARTIES
(THE POLICE, SEPT....THE MENTAL HEALTH SERVICES,
SOUTH ESSEX HOMES....THE HOUSING ASSOCIATION
THAT OWNS THE BUILDING MY FLAT'S IN,
SOUTHEND BOROUGH COUNCIL,
THE FIRE SERVICE, THREE GP'S,
THE MANUFACTURERS OF THE FIRE DOORS,
THE PETROL STATION STAFF, LILLO'S SISTER
AND VARIOUS OTHER WITNESSES)
AND GET ALL THE RELEVANT INFORMATION
AND HOLD PRE-INQUEST HEARINGS,
PLUS THE DELAYS CAUSED BECAUSE
THE BOOKED JUDGE AND PREMISES
WERE UNAVAILABLE,
ALONG WITH THE OUTBREAK OF COVID,
THE ENSUING LOCKDOWNS AND LIMITED ACCESS
TO THE REQUIRED BUILDINGS,
MEANT **I HAD TO WAIT *FIVE YEARS***
FOR THE INQUEST TO FINALLY TAKE PLACE.

THAT HALF A DECADE WAS FRAUGHT WITH WORRY.
ALL I COULD THINK ABOUT WAS,
WHAT SHOULD I SAY? WHAT SHOULD I DO?
HOW CAN WE PREVENT THIS HAPPENING AGAIN?
WHAT WOULD KHABI WANT?

SUCH HEAVY PRESSURE TO GET EVERYTHING RIGHT
AND NOT MISS ANYTHING OUT!

I DIDN'T WANT TO LET ANYONE DOWN.

MY PARANOIA WAS AT ITS WORST AND
THE FEAR AND PRESSURE WAS IMMENSE.
I SO WANTED TO DO THE RIGHT THING,
FOR KHABI AND KaRa,
FOR MY MUM AND KHABI'S MUM
AND THE REST OF THE FAMILY,
FOR HER FRIENDS, FOR THE COMMUNITY,
FOR THE WORLD, EVEN,
BUT IT WAS ALL SO SCARY
AND OVERWHELMING.

I DIDN'T WANT *ANY* OF THIS, REALLY.
I DIDN'T WANT TO MAKE PEOPLE FEEL GUILTY
WHO HAD JUST MADE GENUINE MISTAKES.
I DIDN'T WANT TO GET ANYONE INTO TROUBLE.
I JUST WANTED TO MAKE A DIFFERENCE
SO AS TO PREVENT FURTHER HARM
AND TO MAKE SOMETHING GOOD
COME FROM SUCH AN AWFUL SITUATION.

I WROTE DOWN ALL THE THINGS I WANTED TO ASK.
I MADE NOTES ON WHAT I KNEW HAD HAPPENED.
I THOUGHT ABOUT WHO WAS IN ANY WAY INVOLVED
WHO COULD HAVE DONE THINGS DIFFERENTLY
WHICH MAY HAVE LEAD TO A DIFFERENT OUTCOME.

EVERY TIME SOME NEW PIECE OF INFORMATION
CAME TO LIGHT OR I THOUGHT OF A NEW QUESTION
OR WANTED TO PUT THINGS DIFFERENTLY OR MORE
CONCISELY, I WROTE NEW SETS OF NOTES.
I ENDED UP WITH LITERALLY BAGS OF NOTES,
PIE CHARTS AND FLOW CHARTS OF EVENTS.

IT CONSUMED ME.
I THOUGHT ABOUT IN THE BATH, IN BED,
WHILE EATING, WHILE I WAS OUT, ALL THE TIME!

MY WEIGHT CONTINUED TO PLUMMET,
WHILST MY STRESS LEVELS SKY-ROCKETED.
PEOPLE WERE COMING UP TO ME,
SOME FEELING MY SHOULDERS, TELLING ME,
"OOOH, YOUV'E LOST A LOT OF WEIGHT!"
"YOU NEED TO START EATING MORE!"

AS IF I DIDN'T KNOW!
AS IF I WASN'T ALREADY WORRIED ABOUT IT!
AS IF IT WAS AS EASY AS JUST EATING MORE!
AS IF BEING TOLD THIS
AND HAVING MY BONES GROPED
WASN'T ADDING TO MY STRESS AND WORRY!

I KNEW THEY WERE JUST CONCERNED
BECAUSE THEY CARE ABOUT ME,
BUT IT WAS HARD TO HEAR ALL THE TIME.
AND THE MORE YOU WORRY ABOUT YOUR WEIGHT,
THE MORE IT SEEMS TO GO THE WRONG WAY.

ITS LIKE HAIR-LOSS;
THE MORE YOU WORRY ABOUT GOING BALD,
THE MORE HAIR FALLS FROM YOUR HEAD,
CAUSED *BY* THE WORRY! TALKING OF HAIR-LOSS,
STRESS ALWAYS SEEMS TO AFFECT MY SCALP,
WHICH BROKE OUT IN SCALES
MAKING MY ROOTS GET THIN, MAKING MY
ANKLE-LENGTH DREADLOCKS FEEL EXTRA HEAVY.

WHEN COVID HIT THE NEWS
AND THE WORLD WAS SENTENCED TO LOCKDOWN,
QUITE IRONICALLY, I FOUND IT TO BE THE BREAK
I DESPERATELY NEEDED.

IT POSTPONED THE INQUEST AGAIN,
WHICH GAVE ME A CHANCE TO STOP THINKING
ABOUT WHAT I SHOULD DO AND SAY,
WHICH WAS *AB-SO-LUTE-LY GOLDEN!*
IT ALSO MEANT THAT THERE WERE
DRAMATICALLY FEWER PEOPLE OUT
WHEN I NEEDED TO GO OUT OR WALK THE DOG.
I RELISHED THE ALONE-NESS!

NO QUESTIONS ABOUT THE CASE.
NO BUMPING INTO PEOPLE
WHO HADN'T HEARD ABOUT KHABI
AND NEEDED FILLING IN.
NO ACCUSATIONS OR IMPLICATIONS.
NO DIGGING AT MY RIBS.

ALSO, THERE WAS NONE OF THE USUAL
LAUGHING AND POINTING AT MY HAT OR MY BEARD.
NO BEARD SNIFFING, NO BEARD PULLING,
NO HAIR BEING FELT AND NO RACIST COMMENTS
OR DISGUSTED LOOKS...WHICH WAS NICE!

IT GAVE ME A CHANCE TO PUT THE LAPTOP AWAY.
ALONG WITH ALL THE FILES OF THE JURY BUNDLE
AND THE SUBMISSIONS OF THE INTERESTED PARTIES.
I COULD BREATHE OUT AND RELAX...MIND AND BODY!

THE INQUEST WAS TERRIBLY DELAYED,
BUT THIS WAS ACTUALLY A BLESSING IN DISGUISE,
BECAUSE IT GAVE ME A CHANCE TO FIND OUT
MORE RELEVANT INFORMATION
TO BE BROUGHT UP IN MY QUESTIONS.
IT ALSO GAVE ME TIME TO HEAL SOMEWHAT,
GIVING ME THE STRENGTH TO ENDURE THE INQUEST,
WHICH WAS SET TO LAST ELEVEN DAYS.

AT THE TIME OF THE INQUEST,
I WAS STILL STRUGGLING TO EAT.
TO GET TO THE INQUEST ON TIME,
I GOT UP AT 6:30, GRABBED A SAMOSA,
THE ONLY VEGAN FOOD AVAILABLE
AT THE TRAIN STATION,
A BANANA AND SOME WATER ON THE WAY.
THE SAMOSA MADE ME FEEL ILL,
BECAUSE OF THE OIL IN IT,
SO I PUT IT BACK IN MY BAG
AND GOT THERE HUNGRY.

I HAD SOME SANDWHICHES WITH ME,
BUT NOBODY DARE EAT ANYTHING TOO HEAVY,
IN CASE IT MADE THEM NEED THE TOILET,
WHICH WOULD DELAY THE PROCEEDINGS
OF THE INQUEST, OR CAUSE SOMEONE TO MISS
SOME IMPORTANT PIECE OF INFORMATION.

ALL AROUND THE COURT YOU COULD HEAR
THE FAINT GURGLES OF HUNGRY BELLIES.
MINE INCLUDED.

THE CORONERS' COURT BEGAN AT 10AM EACH DAY,
GOING THROUGH 'TIL AROUND 4 OR 5, SOMETIMES 6 PM.
I'D GET HOME AROUND 9PM, EAT A LITTLE FOOD,
ADJUST MY NOTES AND GO TO BED,
HAVING ONLY HAD A FEW BITES OF FOOD ALL DAY.
BY THE END OF THE TWO WEEKS,
I WAS EXHAUSTED AND MY CLOTHES
WERE HANGING OFF ME.

LIKE I SAID EARLIER, FEAR AND PARANOIA
WERE WREAKING HAVOC IN MY MIND.
THE FRIDAY OF THE FIRST WEEK
WAS FRIDAY THE 13TH.
I WAS SO SCARED THAT SOMEONE
MIGHT WANT TO KILL ME, I THOUGHT,
"WHAT IF THEY TRY TO CRASH MY TRAIN!?!"
SO I DELIBERATELY MISSED MY USUAL TRAIN.

I TOLD MY BARRISTER HOW I FELT,
DURING A BREAK IN THE INQUEST.
HE RE-ASSURED ME THAT NO ONE
WOULD BE TAKING ANY OF THIS PERSONALLY.
HE ALSO SUGGESTED I SOUGHT
SOME PROFESSIONAL COUNSELLING.
NONE THE LESS, I STARTED TO BREAK DOWN
AND HURRIED TO THE TOILETS SO NO ONE SAW ME CRY,
AWAY FROM THE EYES OF ALL THE PEOPLE.
AS THE INQUEST PROGRESSED, THOUGH,
I BEGAN TO FEEL BETTER AND BETTER.
WHEN IT WAS OVER, TO SAY I WAS RELIEVED
WOULD BE THE UNDERSTATEMENT OF THE DECADE!!!

ALTHOUGH...
...IT HADN'T ENDED
WITHOUT KHABI MAKING HER PRESENCE FELT!

I HAD BECOME SO DRAINED
FROM STRESS AND NOT EATING PROPERLY,
THAT I WAS EXHAUSTED AND
I ACTUALLY FOUND MYSELF NODDING OFF
IN THE INQUEST!

I WAS HORRIFIED!
THIS WAS SO IMPORTANT,
BUT, YOU KNOW WHAT IT'S LIKE
WHEN YOUR BODY'S GOING TO SLEEP
WHETHER YOU LIKE IT OR NOT.
THEN SUDDENLY...I WAS OUT!!!
I DON'T KNOW HOW LONG MY EYES
HAD ACTUALLY BEEN CLOSED, BUT,
I JUMPED AWAKE...
...STARTLED BY A TAP ON MY SHOULDER!
I FELT SO ASHAMED!

I TURNED TO MY RIGHT,
EXPECTING TO SEE
A VERY DISAPPOINTED BARRISTER...
...BUT HE WAS STILL SEATED QUITE FAR FROM ME
AND TOTALLY UNAWARE OF MY SITUATION.
I SPUN AROUND...NO ONE WAS THERE!
THINK WHAT YOU WILL...
...I KNOW SOMEONE IN SPIRIT TAPPED MY SHOULDER!
[MORE ON THIS IN THE NEXT CHAPTER!]

SO, I'D SET OUT TO GET ANSWERS
AND MAKE A CHANGE TO THE SYSTEM,
TRYING TO MAKE THE WORLD A LITTLE SAFER
AND GET A LITTLE BIT OF JUSTICE FOR KHABI AND KaRa.

SOME OF THE ANSWERS I GOT
WERE NOT WHAT I WANTED TO HEAR,
BUT WHAT YOU HAVE TO REMEMBER
IN AN INQUEST INTO A DEATH,
IS THAT IT IS ALL LARGELY GUESS WORK,
BECAUSE, IN MANY CIRCUMSTANCES,
WE MAY NEVER KNOW EXACTLY WHAT HAPPENED
ON THE DAY IN QUESTION.

IT WAS ALL VERY
UPSETTING AND FRUSTRATING.
IN THE END, THOUGH,
WE DID MANAGE TO MAKE A DIFFERENCE,
AS A RESULT OF THE INVESTIGATIONS I REQUESTED:

THE MENTAL HEALTH SERVICES
SET UP WHAT THEY CALLED
A "SHARED CARE AGREEMENT",
WHICH MEANS THERE WILL BE
A TRAINED MENTAL HEALTH NURSE PRESENT
IN ALL LOCAL GP SURGERIES, MEANING
IF THERE WAS EVER AN ISSUE WITH THE CARE
BEING GIVEN TO A PATIENT, THERE WOULD BE
APPROPRIATE STAFF AVAILABLE
TO INTERVENE AND PROVIDE
APPROPRIATE CARE.

ALSO, THE POLICE CREATED DESIGNATED TEAMS
TO HANDLE SIMILAR CASES, SO AS TO ENSURE
SOMEONE LIKE LILLO WOULD NOT
SLIP THROUGH THE CRACKS,
ENSURING THEIR DETAILS WOULD BE
BETTER CIRCULATED AND FOLLOWED UP ON.

THE PICTURE THAT EMERGED
FROM ALL THE QUESTIONING
OF THE INQUEST, WAS THAT
A CATALOGUE OF ERRORS
AND FAILURES HAD OCURRED
LEADING TO LILLO'S BREAK-DOWN
AND KHABI AND KaRa'S DEATHS.

THE POLICE, MENTAL HEALTH SERVICES,
GP'S, SOUTHEND BOROUGH COUNCIL AND
OTHERS HAD ALL MADE HONEST MISTAKES.

"LESSONS HAVE BEEN LEARNED"
IS THE BASIC RESPONSE FROM ALL PARTIES...
...BUT, SURELY, THESE LESSONS WERE OBVIOUS
AND SHOULD HAVE BEEN LEARNED DECADES AGO!?!

ALL THIS BEING SAID, THE STARK REALITY IS
THAT THIS ALL *COULD* HAPPEN AGAIN.
EVEN THE CORONER FELT THIS WAS THE CASE!

HOWEVER...<u>THERE'S NO ACTUAL BLAME ON ANYONE</u>,
AS THE *REAL* BAD GUY IN ALL THIS...
...THE ONE WHO ALLOWED THIS PAIN TO BE FELT...

...IS THE VERY SAME CULPRIT
WHO HAS CAUSED PAIN IN EVERYONE'S LIVES;
THE ONE WHO THREATENS OUR EXISTANCE...
...AND THE EXISTANCE OF ANIMALS,
PLANTS, FISH, VEGETABLES, ETC...
...THE ONE BEHIND ALL THE IVORY POACHING;
THE ONE BEHIND CRUELTY;
THE ONE BEHIND SLAVERY;
THE ONE BEHIND CORRUPTION;
THE ONE BEHIND NEARLY ALL SUFFERING...
...OF HUMANS AND ANIMALS ALIKE;
THE ONE BEHIND NEARLY EVERY SINGLE CRIME;
THE ONE WHO THREATENS
THE VERY PLANET WE DEPEND UPON
FOR SUSTENANCE AND HABITATION;
THE ONE BEHIND GREED AND MONOPOLY;
THE ONE KEEPING CERTAIN COUNTRIES
POOR AND UNDERDEVELOPED;
THE ONE BEHIND CLOSING
MENTAL HEALTH HOSPITALS,
COMMUNITY CENTRES
AND OTHER BUSINESSES IN GENERAL;
THE ONE THAT LIMITS SERVICES
AND THE QUALITY OF THEIR SERVICE;
THE ONE THAT PUTS THE WRONG PEOPLE
IN THE WRONG JOB, FOR THE WRONG REASONS;
THE ONE THAT CONTROLS OUR LIVES AND
FORCES US TO MAKE SACRIFICES;
THE ONE THAT FORCES WOMEN
TO SELL THEIR BODIES;
THE ONE BEHIND PAID ASSASSINS, ETC...

...THIS EVIL ONE HAS MANY NAMES,
BUT THE GENERAL NAME GIVEN IS...
...MONEY!!!
"FILTHY LUCRE",
TRULY, THE ROOT OF ALL EVIL. MAM<u>MON</u>(EY)!

SOME WILL SAY, "NO, ITS THE LOVE OF MONEY
THAT IS THE ROOT OF ALL EVIL."
TO WHICH I SHALL SAY, "NO...
...IT'S THE VERY EXISTANCE OF MONEY
THAT IS THE ROOT OF ALL EVIL...
...BECAUSE AS SOON AS YOU ASCRIBE
MONETARY VALUE TO A THING,
THERE INSTANTLY BECOMES THOSE WITHOUT IT.
IT CREATES A LACK. IT CREATES A NEED,
WHEN THERE WAS NO LACK OR NEED
BEFORE ITS CREATION.

A LACK OF FUNDING HAD POLICE
OVER-STRETCHED AND UNDER-STAFFED.
THEY WERE EXTREMELY BUSY WITH CRIME,
MOST OF WHICH WAS BEING COMMITTED DUE TO
A NEED, OR GREED, FOR MONEY.
A LACK OF FUNDING LIKELY MEANT THAT
THE MENTAL HEALTH SERVICES
STAFF DID NOT HAVE THE TIME
TO PROPERLY FAMILIARIZE THEMSELVES WITH
THE CLIENTS HISTORY AND BACKGROUND,
LEADING TO POOR ASSESSMENT
AND POOR QUALITY OF THE SERVICE.
THE SAME IS TRUE FOR THE GP'S.

CLOSED HOSPITALS MEANT THAT
LILLO HAD TO LIVE IN A COMMUNITY
THAT CAUSED HIM PAIN:-
HE WAS BULLIED AND/OR HARRASSED BY PEOPLE AND
SEEMS TO'AVE STRUGGLED TO COPE WITH LIFE PROPERLY.

FURTHERMORE, BECAUSE MONEY HAS BECOME
THE NUMBER ONE PRIORITY IN OUR LIVES,
LOVE HAS TAKEN A BACK SEAT AND TIME IS MONEY,
SO THERE'S NO TIME FOR BEING CARE-FULL,
SO, APPARENTLY, NOT ENOUGH WAS DONE
WHEN PEOPLE SAW HOW THIS MAN WAS LIVING;
WHEN THEY SAW HOW THIN HE WAS GETTING;
WHEN THEY HEARD THAT HE WAS NOT
BEING GIVEN THE CORRECT MEDICATION;
WHEN THEY KNEW THEY COULD NOT
PROVIDE HIM WITH THE RIGHT MEDICATION;
WHEN THEY HEARD THE CONCERNS OF HIS FAMILY,
OF HIS GP, OF HIS NEIGHBOURS....OF OURS.

THIS *IS* A REAL REASON....BUT NOT AN EXCUSE.
THERE ARE MANY PEOPLE LIVING IN POVERTY,
WHO ARE FAR FROM UN-CARING!
THEY ARE LOVE MILLIONAIRES, IN FACT!
WHY IS IT THAT THE POOREST PEOPLE ARE USUALLY
THE WARMEST AND MOST SHARING PEOPLE,
WHILE THE RICHEST PEOPLE SEEM TO USUALLY BE
THE COLDEST, MEANEST AND MOST STRESSED PEOPLE!?!
WHEN MONEY DIES...JUSTICE AND FREEDOM,
RIGHTEOUSSNESS AND LOVE SHALL RISE AGAIN
AND PEOPLE WILL BE FREE TO LIVE BETTER,
STAYING HAPPIER AND HEALTHIER AS A RESULT.

WHILST WRITING THIS BOOK,
I LEARNED LILLO WAS TO BE GRANTED
TIME ALONE IN THE COMMUNITY,
WHICH SOON PROGRESSED TO BEING ALLOWED
TO SPEND DAYS AWAY FROM THE UNIT...
...*WITHOUT SUPERVISION!*

AS YOU CAN IMAGINE,
I WENT MAD EVERY STEP OF THE WAY!
I POURED OUT MY EMOTIONS
REGARDING HOW THIS MADE ME FEEL,
TO LILLO'S PROBATION OFFICERS,
WHO TOLD ME THAT THEY DID NOT HAVE
THE POWER TO MAKE THE CHANGES
I WAS REQUESTING BE MADE.

I TOLD THEM I UNDERSTOOD THAT,
BUT THAT I EXPECTED THEM TO PASS ON MY VIEWS
TO THE PEOPLE WHO *COULD* MAKE A DIFFERENCE.
THEY DID THIS, BUT I HAVEN'T HEARD ANY RESPONSE.
I STILL HAVE TO CHASE THIS UP.

ANOTHER ISSUE REVEALED BY ALL THIS – AND FROM
WHAT I SAW WHILST DOING VOLUNTARY YOUTH WORK -
IS THAT (LARGELY BLACK) CHILDREN ARE BEING TAGGED
FOR STEALING, WHILE MURDERERS WALK FREELY.

I THINK THEY SHOULD TAKE ALL THE TAGS
OFF ALL THESE KIDS' LEGS
AND PUT THEM ON THE KILLERS,
RAPISTS AND PAEDOPHILES.

THESE ARE THE ONES WHO NEED
THEIR LOCATION TO BE KNOWN
AND THEIR MOVEMENTS RESTRICTED;
*ROBBERS OF LIFE, SAFETY AND INNOCENCE,
NOT ROBBERS OF MONEY OR PROPERTY.*
WHERE IS THE SENSE? WHERE IS THE LOVE?
WHERE IS THE RESPECT FOR LIFE AND MORALITY
THAT THE SYSTEM SAVES FOR MONEY AND MATERIAL?

WHERE IS THE LEARNING?
**LILLO DID WHAT HE DID BECAUSE
HE WAS LEFT UNCARED FOR/UNSUPERVISED,**
WHICH CREATED THE OPPORTUNITY FOR HIM
TO GO UN-MEDICATED WITHOUT DETECTION
OR RESOLUTION FOR ALMOST A YEAR AND A HALF.
NOW HE'S BEING LEFT TO HIS OWN DEVICES *AGAIN!*

TO MY MIND,
AS SOON AS HE WALKS OUT THE DOOR OF THE UNIT,
CARE FOR HIM, CARE FOR THE COMMUNITY
AND CARE FOR KHABI AND KaRa CEASE.
FORGET ABOUT CARE FOR JUSTICE.

LILLO COULD DO ANYTHING IN THE TIME
HE IS GIVEN IN THE COMMUNITY.
HE COULD KILL SOMEONE AGAIN.

HE COULD KILL HIMSELF, EVEN,
AS I KNOW HE FEELS TERRIBLY SORRY
SINCE BEING GIVEN HIS MEDICATION
AND REALISING WHAT HE'S DONE!

**HE HAS BEEN EXCLUDED FROM MY AREA,
BUT THAT'S NO COMFORT OR PENALTY.**
WHO'S TO SAY HE'S EVEN GOING TO ABIDE BY THIS?
**WHAT ABOUT THE SAFETY OF THE PEOPLE THAT LIVE
IN THE AREA HE *IS* ALLOWED TO FREQUENT!?!**

I ATTENDED A CHARITY EVENT,
WHERE I MET WITH OTHER FAMILIES
WHO HAD LOST LOVED ONES
AT THE HANDS OF PEOPLE
WITH MENTAL HEALTH ISSUES.

I MET A LADY WHO'D LOST HER SON,
WHEN A MAN, WHO HAD BEEN
EXCLUDED FROM HIS ORIGINAL AREA
AND RESTRICTED TO WHERE HER SON LIVED
- AND WAS NOT BEING MONITORED -
BECAME SO UNWELL
AS TO SMASH HER SONS' HEAD IN, WITH A HAMMER.

CLEARLY MORE NEEDS TO BE DONE,
THAN JUST CREATING EXCLUSION ZONES!
**WHAT'VE WE TAUGHT LILLO (AND THE WORLD)?
WE HAVE SHOWN HIM THAT
HE CAN GET AWAY WITH MURDER, FOR
WE HAVE REWARDED CRIME WITH CARE.**
WE HAVE TAUGHT HIM TO OFFEND
TO GET THE CARE HE NEEDS.

**INSTEAD OF CARE BEING THE LAST RESORT,
MORE PEOPLE (AND LEADERS AND GOVERNORS)
NEED TO START PUTTING LOVE FIRST!**

CHAPTER 10...MIRACLES MEANWHILE!

SO WE'RE AGREED...THE WORLD NEEDS TO CHANGE!

LOVE
MUST LEAD!
FOR THIS TO HAPPEN,
THERE MUST BE A CHANGE
IN THE COLLECTIVE MINDSET.
THERE MUST BE UNIVERSAL UPLIFTMENT.

I HOPE THE HONEST-TO-GOD TRUTH
I SHARE WITH YOU IN THIS BOOK
CHANGES OR UPLIFTS YOU,
MAKING FOR A BETTER EXPERIENCE
OF THIS WORLD
FOR US ALL!
I TOLD YOU ALREADY,
OF THE SIGNS MY "STEP"DAD HAD GIVEN
THAT PROVED TO ME
THAT THERE REALLY IS NO END TO LIFE...
...WELL...THERE'S MORE!

IT WAS KHABI'S TURN TO SHOW US SIGNS!
MY BREDRIN, JASON, KNEW THERE WOULD BE SIGNS.
HE SAID, "BE STILL AND THEY WILL COME"...
...AND THEY *DID!*
WHAT FOLLOWS PROVES THAT
WHEREVER KHABI IS...SHE *IS THERE!*
SHE'S POWERFUL!
SHE'S ALIVE!

I'LL TRY MY BEST
TO GET THINGS IN THE RIGHT ORDER,
BUT I CAN'T FORGET HOW IT ALL STARTED!!!

PROOF THAT KHABI WAS INDEED STILL WITH ME BEGAN WITH THE MOST SPECTACULAR SIGN
I'VE EVER HAD IN MY LIFE.
THE MOST IMPORTANT TYPE OF SIGN...
...A *PHYSICAL* ONE! PHYSICAL PROOF!

AN ACTUAL MIRACLE BY ANYONE'S STANDARDS!

I NEED TO GIVE YOU THE HISTORY FIRST.
WHILST WE WERE LIVING IN AFRICA, **IN 2010,**
I BEGAN TO EXPERIENCE A PAIN IN MY CHEST,
EITHER IN MY HEART OR IN MY LEFT LUNG,
WHEN I'D GO TO BED AND LAY ON MY LEFT SIDE.

I COULD LAY ON MY RIGHT OR ON MY BACK FINE,
BUT WHEN I WOULD TURN ONTO MY LEFT SIDE,
AFTER ABOUT A MINUTE, IT WOULD START TO HURT.
IT FELT LIKE A HOLLY LEAF IN MY CHEST.

IT WAS SO UNCOMFORTABLE.
IT WOULD BECOME UNBEARABLE
AND I WOULD HAVE TO TURN ONTO MY RIGHT SIDE
TO MAKE THE PAIN STOP AND GET BACK TO SLEEP.
IF I ROLLED ONTO MY LEFT SIDE IN MY SLEEP,
IT WOULD SOON WAKE ME UP,
IT WAS THAT BAD.

DURING THE WEEK LEADING UP TO THE FIRE, COMPLETELY OUT OF THE BLUE, **KHABI ASKED ME, "DO YOU STILL GET THAT PAIN IN YOUR CHEST?"**

"YEAH!", I SAID.

"DON'T WORRY ABOUT THAT!", SHE GOES, **"I'M GONNA HEAL THAT FOR YOU!"**

"YEAH!!!???", I SAID, QUITE SUPRISED.

"YEAH, THAT'S MY NEXT....(Pauses)....THING!"

"OK! BLESS!", I SAID, THINKING *SHE COULD DO IT!*
THEN NO MORE WAS SAID ABOUT IT
AND I THOUGHT NO MORE OF IT.

THEN....**THREE DAYS AFTER HER BODY HAD DIED, I WOKE UP, LYING ON MY LEFT SIDE... ...WITH NO PAIN!!!**

I COULDN'T BELIEVE IT!
I EVEN TRIED LAYING ON MY LEFT
TO SEE IF IT WOULD HURT....IT DIDN'T!
THAT NIGHT, WHEN I WENT TO BED
I LAYED ON MY LEFT SIDE
AND, AGAIN, THERE WAS NO PAIN.
IT HASN'T HURT ME SINCE.
I HAD SUFFERED WITH IT FOR SIX YEARS!
SEVEN YEARS LATER, STILL NO PAIN!
SHE KEPT HER PROMISE....IN THE SPIRIT REALM!

**THIS IS PHYSICAL EVIDENCE THAT LIFE
CONTINUES BEYOND THE VEIL OF DEATH.**

KHABI'S BODY IS DEAD...
...BUT SOME ASPECT OF HER CLEARLY STILL EXISTS
AND IS ABLE TO MAKE AN IMPACT
ON THIS PHYSICAL REALM.

ONE NIGHT, I WOKE UP IN THE EARLY HOURS
AND COULD HEAR THE FLOORBOARDS CREAKING,
EVEN THOUGH NO ONE WAS THERE.
THE NEXT MORNING,
THERE WAS A WHITE FEATHER ON THE FLOOR,
NEXT TO THE BED.

EVEN WHEN THE INQUEST BEGAN,
I WAS FULL OF NERVES AND FEARS.
I WALKED DOWN THE PLATFORM,
TURNED AND OPENED THE DOOR
AND THERE ON THE FLOOR OF THE CARRIAGE
WAS A WHITE FEATHER!

THEN, WHILE KHABI'S BROTHER, LEFA,
AND PARENTS, SAM AND NONKY,
WERE OVER FOR THE FUNERAL,
NONKY TOLD ME THAT SHE'D
HAD A DREAM OF KHABI.

I ASKED HER WHAT HAPPENED IN THE DREAM.
SHE SAID SHE SAW KHABI SITTING IN A BASKET
AND THAT SHE WAS WAVING AT HER,
LIKE SHE WAS SAYING GOODBYE!

I COULDN'T BELIEVE WHAT I WAS HEARING...
...BECAUSE I KNEW I HAD CHOSEN A COFFIN
MADE OF WOVEN WILLOW STICKS,
JUST LIKE A BASKET! SEE PIC ON P. 74.
SHE WAS AS AMAZED WHEN I TOLD HER THIS.

HOWEVER, THE *VERY* FIRST SIGN
(WHICH I DIDN'T FIND OUT 'TIL LATER)
WAS ACTUALLY THE TIME THE FIRE SERVICES
WERE CALLED THE NIGHT OF THE FIRE....11:11PM!

TO ME, 11 11 REPRESENTS SPIRITUAL COMPANY.
I SEE THE 11'S AS PAIRS OF FEET;
YOUR OWN FOOTPRINTS
NEXT TO TWO "FOOTPRINTS IN THE SAND".

SEVERAL TIMES, JUST PRIOR TO THE FIRE,
KHABI HAD BEEN SEEING THIS TIME ON THE CLOCK
AND HAD BEEN COMMENTING ON IT,
AS SHE HAD BEEN READING ABOUT
IT'S SPIRITUAL SIGNIFICANCE.

THEN THERE WAS THE DATE KHABI'S BODY DIED,
09/05/16....OUR 8TH ANNIVERSARY,
JUST TWO DAYS AFTER
THE FIRE HAD BEEN SET, ON 07/05/16.

THEN, 1 YEAR, 1 MONTH AND 1 WEEK AFTER THE FIRE,
WAS THE TRAGIC GRENFEL FIRE, IN LONDON: 14/06/17.
THAT SAME DAY (14/06/17)...KHABI'S AUNTY DIED
IN AFRICA...WHOSE NICKNAME...WAS *"FIRE"!!!*

I ALSO HAD DREAM-VISIONS OF KHABI.
I CALL THEM DREAM-VISIONS
AS THEY'RE MORE THAN MERE DREAMS...
...I'VE ACTUALLY BEEN MEETING WITH HER
IN SOME KIND OF DREAMLAND!

THE FIRST "DREAM" BEGAN WITH ME
STEPPING OFF A BUS IN TOWN.
AS I LOOKED AROUND ME
I NOTICED HOW
IT WAS A PARTICULARLY BEAUTIFUL DAY.
THE GREEN OF THE LEAVES ON THE TREES
WAS SO VIVID AND THE SUN WAS SO BRIGHT.

I ACTUALLY WONDERED IF I WAS DREAMING
AND RAN A FEW CHECKS:
I'M BREATHING, I'M THINKING.
I SCANNED MY SURROUNDINGS
ALL SEEMED CORRECT,
EVEN THOUGH THE PLACE WAS
HOW IT WAS IN THE 80'S,
AS THE BUS NO LONGER STOPS
WHERE IT DID IN MY VISION.

AS I TURNED, LOOKING AROUND ME,
THE BUS I'D JUST ALIGHTED CAME INTO VIEW...
...AND KHABI CAME STEPPING OUT THE BUS,
HER FACE AND EYES LIT UP BY HER SMILE!
I WAS *SO* PLEASED TO SEE HER!
I HAD FORGOTTEN HOW IT *FELT*
TO BE IN HER PRESENCE:

INNER HAPPINESS, COMPLETENESS, WARMTH, JOY,
EXCITEMENT AND MORE...IT ALL CAME BACK...
...BECAUSE *KHABI WAS BACK!*
THAT FEELING'S NOT SOMETHING REMEMBERED,
IT'S SOMETHING EXPERIENCED LIVE,
IN THE FLESH, AS IT WERE.

WE CROSSED THE ROAD AND
AS SOON AS WE REACHED THE PAVEMENT,
WE EMBRACED ONE ANOTHER AND,
AS I HELD HER IN MY ARMS,
AWARE THAT I COULD FEEL HER IN MY ARMS,
EVEN THOUGH SHE HAD "DIED",
I HOPED I WOULD NEVER FORGET THIS MOMENT!

ANOTHER TIME I SAW HER IN A VISION,
SHE WAS SURROUNDED IN A GOLDEN LIGHT!
I CALLED ONE OF HER FRIENDS, SHERELY,
SOME DAYS LATER, TO SEE HOW SHE WAS COPING.
I ASKED HER IF SHE'D HAD ANY SIGNS FROM KHABI.
SHE TOLD ME SHE'D SEEN HER IN DREAMS.
SHE SAID SHE LOOKED HAPPY...
...*AND WAS SURROUNDED IN A GOLDEN LIGHT!*
JUST LIKE HOW I SAW HER IN MY "DREAM"!
**THE FACT THAT WE BOTH SAW THE SAME THING
PROVES THAT IT WAS A REAL VISION OF KHABI!**

IN ANOTHER DREAM,
KHABI WAS BUSY PACKING A BAG.
I DON'T KNOW WHERE SHE WAS GOING,
BUT I ASKED HER, "CAN YOU SEE ME FROM THERE?"

"NO", SHE SAID...BUT I KNEW SHE DIDN'T MEAN IT,
'COS SHE WAS CAGEY WHEN SHE SAID IT.
SHE'S SUCH AN HONEST PERSONALITY,
EVEN IN SPIRIT, SHE STILL FINDS IT HARD TO LIE!

"CAN YOU HEAR ME THERE?", I CONTINUED TO PROBE.

"NO", SHE SAID, AVOIDING MY EYES.

"OH....WELL...I'LL TRY 'N' FIND A WAY
TO GET THROUGH TO YOU!", I VOWED.

I WAS CLEARLY ASKING HER
IF SHE WAS ABLE TO SEE AND HEAR ME
FROM WHERE SHE IS, IN THE SPIRIT REALM.

I BELIEVE SHE WAS JUST SAYING NO,
SO THAT I WOULD FEEL FREE TO GO ON
AND MEET NEW WOMEN.
I THINK THIS BECAUSE IT HAPPENED
AROUND THE TIME I WAS TALKING TO SOMEONE NEW,
SOME YEARS AFTER KHABI HAD RETURNED TO SPIRIT.
UNFORTUNATELY I HAD TOO MANY ISSUES STILL
AND IT SOON FIZZLED OUT.

LET ME TELL YOU
ABOUT ONE MORE DREAM-VISION I HAD OF KHABI:
IT BEGAN WITH ME WAKING UP IN BED,
STRUGGLING TO BREATHE,
SO I MADE MY WAY TO THE WINDOW FOR FRESH AIR.
AS I STOOD AT THE WINDOW...

...KHABI CAME AND STOOD NEXT TO ME!

NOTHING CLICKED IN MY MIND YET.
IT JUST FELT LIKE ANY OTHER DAY.
THEN SHE TOLD ME SHE WAS GOING TO GO BATHE.
I TURNED TO WATCH HER LEAVE.
AS SHE SLINKED OUT THE ROOM,
SHE LOOKED BACK AT ME, SMILING.
THEN I NOTICED A SMALL BURN ON HER BACK
AND I FINALLY REALIZED!

"BABE! YOU'RE BACK!!!", I EXCLAIMED, EXCITEDLY!

"YEAH!", SHE SAID.

"BUT THE FIRE! NOW YOU'RE BACK!"

WITH HER BEAUTIFUL EYES LOOKING DEEP INTO MINE,
WITH A BEAMING SMILE, SHE JUST SAID, "I KNOW!",
IN A WAY THAT SEEMED TO MEAN
IT WAS ALL QUITE INCONSEQUENTIAL!

I JUST RAN AND GAVE HER A BIG SQUEEZE.
WITH MY ANGEL-QUEEN IN MY ARMS, I PRAYED:
"FATHER-MOTHER-GOD, THANK YOU
FOR BRINGING MY QUEEN BACK TO ME!"

AGAIN, I COULD FEEL HER IN MY ARMS AND
I WAS AWARE THAT SHE HAD DIED IN THE WORLD
AND YET, REGARDLESS OF THIS FACT,
HERE WE WERE TOGETHER AGAIN!

THE SIGNS CONTINUE NOW,
EVEN AS I'M WRITING THIS,
I GOT A LITTLE SIGN FROM HER,
LETTING ME KNOW SHE'S HERE!

WHEN I FINISHED WRITING ABOUT THE DREAM,
ON THE PREVIOUS PAGE,
I WAS ABOUT TO CONTINUE TYPING
AND TELL YOU ABOUT A TIME,
WHEN I WAS AT MY MUM'S PLACE,
PLAYING KHABI'S MUSIC PLAYLIST
ON HER TABLET:

WHILE I WAS TALKING TO MUM ABOUT KHABI,
I MENTIONED KHABI'S NAME
AND THE MUSIC PAUSED!
I UNPAUSED IT AND CARRIED ON TALKING,
WITH THE MUSIC PLAYING IN THE BACKGROUND.
I SAID HER NAME AGAIN, IN THE CONVERSATION.
THE MUSIC PAUSED AGAIN!
I UNPAUSED IT, BUT IT HAPPENED A THIRD TIME!

BUT INSTEAD OF TYPING THIS,
I FELT I SHOULD REMIND MY MUM
ABOUT THE DREAM ON THE PREVIOUS PAGE.
I TOLD HER, "I'VE JUST WRITTEN ABOUT THAT DREAM
WHERE I WOKE UP UNABLE TO BREATHE
AND KHABI CAME AND JOINED ME AT THE WINDOW!"
MUM SEEMED DEEPLY MOVED.
THAT SAME MOMENT,
THE MUSIC I WAS PLAYING IN THE BACKGROUND,
AGAIN, FROM KHABI'S PLAYLIST, *PAUSED!!!*

I STOPPED BELIEVING IN COINCIDENCE YEARS AGO.
I'VE NOTICED TOO MUCH PRECISE DESIGN AND
SPIRITUAL INTERVENTION TO IGNORE THE FACT THAT
EVERY SINGLE THING THAT HAPPENS IN LIFE
HAS A REASON AND A SEASON.
NOTHING IS LEFT TO CHANCE!
NOTHING IS ACCIDENTAL.
ALL IS GUIDANCE.

EVEN THE BAD THINGS HAPPEN FOR A REASON.
THEY HAVE THEIR PURPOSE AND TEACHING.
ULTIMATELY THEY MAKE WAY FOR SOMETHING GOOD,
WHETHER FOR EXPERIENCE, KNOWLEDGE, WARNING
OR TO PREVENT SOMETHING EVEN WORSE
FROM HAPPENING, BECAUSE,
REGARDLESS OF HOW BAD THINGS ARE,
THINGS *COULD* BE *EVEN WORSE!*
GIVE THANKS THAT THEY AREN'T.

"COINCIDENCE" IS A COP OUT.
IT IGNORES THE POTENTIAL
FOR DIVINE INTERVENTION.
THAT'S WHAT THE SYSTEM
WANTS YOU TO DO...
...FORGET GOD.
RATHER...FORGET MAN AND HIS LIMITING LANGUAGE.

THE REALITY IS THAT
EVERYTHING IS A GIFT FROM THE CREATOR
AND IN EVERY EXPERIENCE THERE IS A TEACHING;
EVEN IN SLEEPING!

IF WE CAN RECALL OUR DREAMS,
WE'RE BEING REMINDED OF SOMETHING
VERY IMPORTANT.
EACH NIGHT, WE GET TIRED
AND OUR BODY STARTS TO SHUT DOWN.
THE EYELIDS BECOME HEAVY AND BEGIN TO CLOSE
AND NO MATTER HOW MUCH YOU TRY TO STAY AWAKE,
YOUR BODY HAS HAD ENOUGH AND
IT'S GOING TO SLEEP, READY OR NOT!

WE MAY WANT TO STAY AWAKE,
BUT *OUR BODY* DOESN'T!
IT'S SEPARATE FROM US SO IT SLEEPS,
BUT **WHILE IT SLEEPS, WE,
THE NON-BODY PART OF US STAYS AWAKE AND DREAMS!**
THAT PART OF US DOES NOT NEED THE BODY
TO HAVE EXPERIENCES AND INTERACTIONS!
IT'S *THAT* PART OF US SURVIVES THE FLESH-DEATH.
THIS LEADS ME TO THE CONCLUSION THAT THE
"AFTERLIFE" IS A PLACE OF COMMUNAL "DREAMS"!
"DREAM-HEAVEN-REALITY"
I CALLED IT IN MY OTHER BOOK.

NOW, READ THIS BEAUTIFUL QUOTE
FROM A BOOK CALLED,
"WINGED PHARAOH", BY JOAN GRANT.
TO PARAPHRASE:
"….I REMEMBERED THAT SOMETIMES,
WHEN LOOKING ON BRIGHT WATER,
I HAD SEEN VISIONS, AS VIVID AS A TRUE DREAM.
I PRAYED TO PTAH OF HIS COMPASSION
TO CLEAR MY EYES. I LOOKED AT THE LIGHT. . . .

"I SAW MY FATHER – HE WAS SMILING.
STRANGE. . . I COULD HEAR. . . I HEARD HIS VOICE.
HE SAID, 'MY DAUGHTER, TELL YOUR MOTHER THAT,
KNOWING VICTORY, MY BODY DIED FROM A SPEAR,
AND MY SPIRIT LEFT IT LIKE A WILD BIRD
FREED FROM THE SNARE OF THE FOWLER.

'TELL HER TO SLEEP EARLY TO-NIGHT
SO THAT WE MAY WALK HERE TOGETHER,
FOR I HAVE MUCH TO SAY TO HER.

**'TELL HER NOT TO GRIEVE AT MY FREEDOM,
BUT TO SHARE IT WITH ME.**

'TELL HER THAT SHE BUT STEPS
FROM HER SLEEPING BODY TO MY ARMS.' "

* * *

I'VE HAD SEVERAL OTHER DREAM-VISIONS
AND SOME REGULAR DREAMS OF KHABI.
THE DIFFERENCE BETWEEN THE DREAMS AND
THE REAL DREAM-VISIONS
IS BEING AWARE THAT I AM SEEING HER,
EVEN THOUGH SHE'D DIED IN FLESH,
BUT, SOMEHOW, SHE'S HERE WITH ME NOW.
THIS REALIZATION IS USUALLY ACCOMPANIED BY
FEELINGS OF EXTREME SURPRISE AND EXCITEMENT.
IF YOU DON'T DREAM OF PEOPLE YOU HAVE LOST,
DON'T DESPAIR....YOU PROBABLY ARE,
YOU'RE JUST NOT REMEMBERING THEM.

I'VE BEEN TOLD THAT
HIGH LEVELS OF EMOTIONS
CAN BLOCK A SPIRITS' ATTEMPTS
TO COMMUNICATE WITH US.

SO TRY TO BE CALM
AND REMEMBER THE ETERNAL TRUTH.
DON'T TRY TO IMAGINE WHAT KIND OF SIGN
YOU WILL BE GETTING, JUST BE AWARE
AND KEEP AN OPEN MIND.

IT COULD BE ANYTHING.
THEY USUALLY MAKE US NOTICE SOMETHING
THAT HAS A MEANING TO US,
LIKE A NUMBER PLATE, A SONG ON THE RADIO,
A FEATHER, A ROBIN, A BUTTERFLY, ETC...

MY BREDRIN, KEETY, AND HIS FAMILY
TOLD ME THEY KEPT SEING A BUTTERFLY
WITH WHITE SPOTS ON ITS WINGS.
THEN, ONE DAY I WAS CYCLING
AND ONE OF THESE BUTTERFLIES
WAS FLYING ALONG WITH ME,
RIGHT NEXT TO MY FRONT WHEEL.
IT STAYED WITH ME FOR A WHILE,
THEN FLEW OFF.

ANOTHER TIME CYCLING,
ANOTHER ONE OF THESE SPOTTED BUTTERFLIES
FLUTTERED ABOUT RIGHT IN FRONT OF MY FACE
AS I HURTLED ALONG, IT STAYED JUST THERE...THEN
IT DROPPED, BRUSHED MY HAND AND FLEW AWAY!

THE SIGNS ARE CONSTANT AND CONSISTENT.

A GOOD BREDRIN OF MINE, COLLIN,
HAD VERY SUDDENLY RETURNED TO SPIRIT RECENTLY.
I'VE KNOWN HIM SINCE GOING
TO MY FIRST REGGAE DANCES, DURING THE 90'S,
INTRODUCED TO ME BY FRIEND, KATE.

I WENT TO HIS BODY'S FUNERAL,
WHICH WAS AT THE CREMATORIUM,
JUST ACCROSS THE STREET
FROM THE CEMETERY
WHERE KHABI'S BODY WAS PLANTED.

AFTER THE SERVICE, I WAS TALKING
WITH COLLIN'S WIDOW, MARIANNE.
I WAS EXPLAINING TO HER THAT LIFE IS ETERNAL
AND THAT I GET SIGNS FROM KHABI ALL THE TIME.
SHE ASKED ME IF I FEEL KHABI'S SPIRIT AROUND ME.
I TOLD HER I DON'T, BUT I DO GET SIGNS FROM HER,
USUALLY IN THE FORM OF WHITE FEATHERS.

THEN, WHEN SHE LEFT, I DECIDED TO GO
AND VISIT KHABI'S GRAVE QUICKLY.
WHEN I GOT THERE, WHAT DID I FIND???
A WHITE FEATHER NEXT TO THE FLOWERS
I HAD PLACED THERE LAST TIME.

EVEN MY DAD'S GRAVE
WAS COVERED IN WHITE FEATHERS
WHEN I WENT THERE ON HIS BIRTHDAY,
ON CHRISTMAS EVE, THIS YEAR (2022).

BUT MORE SIGNIFICANTLY, SIX DAYS AFTER THAT,
ON KHABI'S BIRTHDAY, 30/12/22,
I DROVE WITH MY MUM TO THE CEMETERY
SO WE COULD LAY SOME FLOWERS.

ON THE WAY, THE RADIO WAS PLAYING IN THE CAR.
I PAID CLOSE ATTENTION TO WHAT WAS PLAYING,
BECAUSE THE PREVIOUS YEAR,
WHEN LEAVING THE CEMETERY,
I SAID I WANTED TO HEAR ADELES, "EASY ON ME".
I TURNED THE RADIO ON...AND WAS SHE PLAYING?
NO! LOOOOOOOOOOL!
I HOPE THAT MADE YOU CHUCKLE!

THE *NEXT* TUNE THAT PLAYED, THOUGH,
WAS INDEED ADELE, SINGING, "EASY ON ME"!
AFTER THAT SONG, I STARTED GOING THROUGH
ALL THE DIFFERENT RADIO STATIONS.
I PICKED UP A REGGAE STATION,
THAT PLAYED A TUNE CALLED, "JOSEPHINE".
THAT'S KHABI'S MIDDLE NAME!

IMAGINE THAT! HEARING KHABI'S NAME
ON THE RADIO
JUST AFTER BEING AT HER BODY'S GRAVE,
ON HER BIRTHDAY!
SO THIS YEAR I PAID CLOSE ATTENTION
TO THE SONGS THAT PLAYED
FOR THE ENTIRE JOURNEY.
JUST AS WE REACHED THE ROAD
THAT LEADS TO THE CEMETERY...

...A REGGAE(-ISH) TUNE PLAYED, CALLED...
"I SAW THE SIGN"!!! THE SONG WAS THE SIGN!

THEN WHILE I WAS AT THE GRAVE,
I WANTED TO PLAY SOME MUSIC OFF MY PHONE.
THE FIRST TUNE THAT CAME UP
WAS A SOUTH AFRICAN TUNE!
"LENGOMA", BY ZAHARA.
LENGOMA MEANS, *THIS SONG!*
THIS SIGN WAS "THIS SONG"!

I LEFT THE TUNE PLAYING IN MY TOP POCKET
WHILST LAYING THE FLOWERS,
LIGHTING THE INCENSE
AND SAYING TWO BLESSINGS.
IT WAS LATE AND GETTING DARK AND
I WAS WORRIED ABOUT GETTING LOCKED IN,
SO I DIDN'T TARRY TOO LONG.

I DID QUICKLY GO TO MY DAD'S GRAVE TO
LIGHT SOME INCENSE THERE, THOUGH.
THE MUSIC WAS STILL PLAYING.
AS I LEFT MY DAD'S GRAVE, "LENGOMA" FINISHED
AND I WONDERED WHAT SONG WOULD PLAY NEXT.

THE PHONE WAS ON SHUFFLE.
THE NEXT TUNE BEGAN...
...I RECOGNIZED IT INSTANTLY...
...I GOT INTO THE CAR AND TOLD MUM TO LISTEN.

ALICIA KEYS SPOKE SOFTLY, SAYING...

..."THIS SONG IS DEDICATED...
...TO ALL THE LOVERS WHO CAN'T BE TOGETHER...
...SEPARATED...BY DISTANCE AND TIME"!

HOW SIGNIFICANT AND POIGNANT CAN YOU GET!?!
BOTH MY MOTHER AND I, SAT JUST YARDS AWAY
FROM EACH OF OUR SOUL-MATES' GRAVES!
IT WAS VERY EMOTIONAL, YET UPLIFTING.

THEN WE DROVE OFF....MUSIC STILL PLAYING.
BUT AS WE WENT, MUM WAS DRIVING SLOWLY,
SAYING SHE COULDN'T SEE PROPERLY.
SHE TOOK HER GLASSES OFF TO CLEAN THEM,
BUT IT MADE NO DIFFERENCE.
SHE SAID SHE'D STARTED HAVING DIFFICULTY
TO SEE WHILE SHE WAS WATCHING ME
PUT THE FLOWERS ON THE GRAVE.

SHE KEPT CLEANING HER GLASSES,
THEN SHE REALIZED...
...SHE COULD SEE BETTER *WITHOUT* HER GLASSES!
IN FACT SHE COULD SEE PERFECTLY.
WE SAT THERE WHILE I ASKED
IF SHE COULD SEE VARIOUS THINGS,
LIKE A SIGN NEARBY, THE ROAD,
THE CARS IN THE DISTANCE.
SHE COULD SEE IT ALL!

THEN I SUDDENLY HEARD THE LYRICS
OF THE NEXT RANDOM SONG PLAYING...
...IT WAS ALICIA KEYS AGAIN...
..."WELL PEOPLE DON'T SEE...WHAT I SEE!"

FOUR SONGS, ALL PERFECTLY RELEVANT
IN VARIOUS WAYS!

NOW LISTEN TO THIS!
MUM AND I HAVE BEEN GOING TO
A SPIRITUALIST CHURCH,
WHERE THEY TEACH TECHNIQUES
OF CONNECTING WITH SPIRITS,
BECAUSE, APPARENTLY,
WE CAN ALL DEVELOP PSYCHIC ABILITY.

SO JUST THE OTHER DAY,
MUM OFFERED TO DO A READING FOR ME.
SHE SAID A PRAYER, ASKING THE SPIRITS
OF OUR LOVED ONES TO DRAW CLOSE.
SHE HELD MY HANDS AND CLOSED HER EYES.
WE SAT SILENTLY FOR A BIT.
I WAS JUST LOOKING OUT THE WINDOW...
...I DIDN'T WANT TO GIVE HER ANY MENTAL CLUES.

SHE FINALLY SAID,
"SORRY, ALL I'M GETTING, IS A STRONG IMAGE
OF THAT EGYPTIAN QUEEN YOU PAINTED!
I DON'T KNOW WHY. THAT'S ALL I CAN SEE."

IT MEANT SO MUCH TO ME!
SHE DIDN'T KNOW WHY IT WAS IMPORTANT,
BUT IT WAS! IT CONFIRMED TO ME
THAT I NEED TO GET PAINTING AGAIN,
BECAUSE I WAS BEING REMINDED
HOW IMPORTANT MY ART WAS TO KHABI!

KHABI HAS ALSO BEEN USING NUMBERS AS A SIGN,
MAKING ME NOTICE DOUBLE NUMBERS A LOT
AND NUMBERS THAT REPRESENT THE DATE WE MET,
9/5, THE DATE OF OUR WEDDING, 11/5
OR THE DATE OF THE FIRE 7/5.

SO WHEN I WAS EXPLAINING TO MUM THAT SHE HAD,
INDEED, JUST PASSED ON A MESSAGE, I SAID,
"WHAT'S THE TIME? I BET IT'S DOUBLE FIGURES!"
SHE TURNED THE TV ON TO SEE THE TIME: 15:55!
THE TV IS A BIT OLD AND TEMPERAMENTAL,
SO THESE DAYS, A FEW SECONDS AFTER YOU
SWITCH IT ON, IT TURNS THE CHANNEL OVER.
I WONDERED WHAT CHANNEL IT WOULD CHANGE TO.
WOULD IT BE A DOUBLE NUMBER!?!

BEFORE I COULD SEE THE CHANNEL'S NUMBER,
I SAW WHAT WAS HAPPENING ON THE SCREEN...
...PEOPLE WERE PAINTING ART ON CANVASES...
...JUST WHAT WE'D BEEN TALKING ABOUT!
IT HAD TURNED OVER TO SKY-ARTS.
THE CHANNEL NUMBER IS 11.
THE DATE WAS THE 11TH.
11, 11! AGAIN!

LASTLY, I HAVEN'T BEEN BACK TO MY FLAT
FOR A LONG TIME. SOME FRIENDS FLAT-SAT FOR ME,
BUT IT WAS FILTHY DIRTY WHEN THEY LEFT,
SO I SOLD A LOAD OF MY BELOVED RECORDS,
BOUGHT SOME FURNITURE AND DONE IT UP A BIT.
IT LOOKS LOVELY NOW. BARE, BUT LOVELY.
I INVITED MUM OVER TO SEE IT.

WHEN SHE ARRIVED I SAID I WANTED TO PRAY.
AS I BEGAN TO PRAY, MUM TURNED TO HER LEFT...
...SHE COULD FEEL KHABI STANDING NEXT TO HER!
THIS WASN'T THE FIRST TIME MUM FELT A SPIRIT
STANDING NEXT TO HER IN THIS FLAT!

ON THE VERY DAY OF THE FIRE,
MUM WAS VISITING US.
SHE WAS IN THE LOUNGE TALKING TO KHABI.
I WAS IN THE KITCHEN DOING SOME FOOD.

WHILST MUM WAS TALKING TO KHABI,
SHE PAUSED AND LOOKED TO HER LEFT...
...SHE SAID SHE COULD FEEL SOMEONE STANDING
BESIDE HER AND THOUGHT IT WAS ME
UNTIL SHE SAW THERE WAS NO ONE THERE!
I RECKON MY DAD HAD DRAWN CLOSE TO US,
IN PREPARATION FOR THE FIRE,
GETTING READY TO GREET KHABI
AND WELCOME HER INTO THE LIGHT!

HE WOULD'VE BEEN THE PERFECT PERSON TO DO THIS
BECAUSE HE IS SUCH A CARING PERSONALITY,
WHO CAN MAKE YOU LAUGH,
WHETHER YOU'RE ANGRY OR SAD!
HE WOULD HAVE KEPT HER CALM
AND MADE SUCH A FUSS OF HER,
LIKE HE USED TO DO FOR ME! THANKS RICK!

ANOTHER EXAMPLE OF A SPIRITUAL PRESENCE
HAPPENED THE NIGHT OF THE FIRE!

THAT NIGHT,
I WAS SELLING MY BOOKS AT A REGGAE DANCE,
TAKING PLACE AT THE SAME VENUE KHABI AND I
HAD ATTENDED, FOR A MEMORIAL DANCE
FOR OUR RASTA BREDRIN, "RED-I".
UNBEKNOWNST TO ME, AT THE DANCE,
WHILE THE FIRE WAS RAGING,
RED-I'S DAUGHTER, RACHEL, ARRIVED AT THE DANCE
AND SHE LATER TOLD ME,
THAT SHE'D SEEN HER DAD'S SPIRIT,
STANDING RIGHT BESIDE ME AT MY STALL!
THERE WAS A LOT OF SPIRITUAL SUPPORT THAT NIGHT.

ANOTHER EXAMPLE OF A SPIRITUAL PRESENCE,
WAS WHEN ANOTHER GOOD RASTA BREDRIN OF OURS,
REECE, PASSED OVER WHILE TRAVELLING IN CAMBODIA.
KEETY HAD MADE A POSTER OF HIM,
FOR A DANCE WE HELD IN HIS MEMORY.
HE BROUGHT THE PICTURE TO OUR BREDRIN,
CLIVE'S PLACE, WHERE HE HUNG THE PICTURE UP
AND PLAYED SOME TUNES FOR HIM.

KEETY PLAYED A TUNE THAT HE HAD TO PULL UP
AND PLAY AGAIN, AS HE SAID REECE HAD BEEN
TELLING HIM HOW MUCH HE LOVED THAT TUNE.

AS HE PLAYED THE TUNE,
HE POINTED AT REECES' PICTURE AND SAID,
"THAT MAN LOVED THIS TUNE!"...
...THAT VERY SAME MOMENT...
...REECES' PICTURE FELL TO THE FLOOR!

IT'S REAL!
THEY REALLY ARE STILL ALIVE,
JUST NOT PHYSICALLY,
AND THEY DO TRY TO COMMUNICATE.

I MENTIONED EARLIER,
THAT I DON'T FEEL THE PRESENCE
OF KHABI'S SPIRIT AROUND ME AT ALL.
HOWEVER,
IN THOSE EARLY DAYS AFTER SHE'D LEFT THE FLESH,
I WAS REALLY HOPING TO BE ABLE TO FEEL HER SPIRIT.

EVERY DAY, I HOPED TO PICK UP THAT SENSE
OF HAVING HER SPIRITUAL COMPANY,
BUT I GOT NOTHING.
I WOULD STILL MYSELF AND TRY TO BECOME
SENSITIVE TO SUBTLE ENERGIES,
BUT TO NO AVAIL.

THEN ONE DAY, MUM WAS TAKING THE DOG
FOR A WALK, DOWN TWO-TREE ISLAND,
A LOCAL NATURE RESERVE.
IT WAS A BEAUTIFUL DAY AND I WENT WITH THEM.
AS WE WALKED ONTO THE GRASS
TOWARDS THE ENTRANCE,
THERE IT WAS!!!

I FELT A SLIGHT PRESSURE ON MY SHOULDERS!
EITHER KHABI WAS WALKING WITH ME,
HANGING ON MY SHOULDERS...
...OR SHE'D SAT KaRa ON THEM!
I WAS SO HAPPY AND RELIEVED!

I *DESPERATELY* WANTED
TO *FEEL* HER PRESENCE AROUND ME!
BUT I WAS NEVER GONNA KID MYSELF.
I HAD TO GENUINELY FEEL SOMETHING.
IT MADE SENSE HER SPIRIT WOULD BE THERE,
BECAUSE SHE LOVED BEING IN TOUCH WITH NATURE,
OFTEN WALKING BAREFOOT IN THE GRASS!

ONE WITH NATURE ON TWO-TREE ISLAND!
SHE WAS PART OF THE BEAUTY OF THE SCENERY!

I WANTED/*NEEDED* MORE, THOUGH.
I WANTED TO FIND A WAY
TO CONNECT WITH HER, PSYCHICLY, AS
I DIDN'T DO WELL AT THE TECHINIQUES TAUGHT
AT THE SPIRITUALIST CHURCH.
I BEGAN COMING ACROSS/BEING GUIDED TO
BOOKS ABOUT MEDIUMSHIP, IN CHARITY SHOPS.
I GOOGLED DIFFERENT TECHNIQUES
OF CONTACTING THE DEPARTED.
I WANTED TO FIND A WAY
TO GET IN TOUCH WITH HER
ANY TIME I WANTED TO.

I READ ABOUT MIRROR-GAZING AND
STARING INTO CANDLE FLAMES,
BUT THEN I READ AN ARTICLE,
I THINK IT WAS ON WIKI HOW,
THAT SEEMED QUITE EASY TO TRY.
IT BASICALLY SAID THAT
WE ARE MOST ABLE TO HAVE
A PSYCHIC CONNECTION
WHEN WE'RE ABOUT TO FALL ASLEEP.

IT ADVISED VISUALISING
THE FACE OF THE PERSON YOU WISH TO SEE,
THEN EMPTYING YOUR MIND AND
CLOSING YOUR EYES TO SLEEP.
THIS WAS MEANT TO LEAD TO
HAVING SOME KIND OF VISION
OF THE LOST LOVED ONE
WHILE SLEEPING.

I HAD TO TRY IT... SO THAT NIGHT, IN BED,
I PICTURED HER BEAUTIFUL FACE IN MY MIND,
THEN AFTER JUST A FEW MOMENTS,
I CLEARED MY MIND AND WENT TO SLEEP.
WHEN I WOKE UP, THE DREAM-VISION
WAS STILL FRESH IN MY MIND!

I WAS WALKING ALONG THE PATH
OUTSIDE MY FLAT, WALKING TOWARDS MUM'S CAR,
BUT I COULDN'T SEE THE CAR CLEARLY,
OR MUM AT ALL...ALL I COULD SEE WAS KHABI,
WAITING FOR ME IN THE FRONT PASSENGER SEAT.
MY EYES WERE JUST FOCUSED ON KHABI,
BUT I NOTICED THAT THE ROUNDED, GREY SEATS
DIDN'T LOOK LIKE THE SEATS IN MUM'S CAR.
I ALSO NOTICED THAT HER HAIR WAS DIFFERENT
AND AS I WALKED CLOSER TO HER, I WAS THINKING,
"OH BLESS, SHE'S HAD HER HAIR DONE!"

THEN I STARTED TO THINK ABOUT
HOW I HADN'T SEEN HER FOR A WHILE...
...THEN I REALIZED SHE'D "DIED"...
...BUT THERE SHE WAS,
SITTING, SMILING TO HERSELF,
GIVING ME A SORT OF SIDE GLANCE,
LIKE THE ONE ON P. 71. THEN I WOKE UP!

THE STRANGE CAR SEATS TURNED OUT TO BE THE
SEATS IN MUM'S **NEXT** CAR, THAT SHE HADN'T GOT YET!
VARIOUS OTHER SIGNS HAVE OCCURRED
THAT ARE DETAILED IN MY OTHER BOOK,
"THE COMFORTER".

CHAPTER 11...THE BABY COMMUNICATES!

EVEN OUR BABY GIRL, KaRa,
HAS BEEN GIVING PLENTY OF SIGNS.
I HAVEN'T HAD ANY DREAMS OF HER,
BUT SHE HAS *DEFINATELY* BEEN IN TOUCH!

FIRST OF ALL, THAT CHILD COULD UNDERSTAND US,
FROM WITHIN THE WOMB!

WE WERE LAYING IN BED ONE MORNING
AND I HAD MY HAND ON KHABI'S BUMP.
I RECKONED KaRa COULD HEAR US,
SO, KEEPING MY HAND ON THE BUMP, I SAID,
"KaRa! IF YOU CAN HEAR ME,
PUT ONE HAND IN THE AIR!"
NOTHING HAPPENED.
"WAIT, SHE CAN'T HEAR ME!", I SAID. THEN,
I PULLED THE DUVET BACK AND BOOMED IN PATOIS,
"MI SEH (ME SAY/I SAID)...IF UNU (YOU) CAN 'EAR ME,
ONE 'AND INNA DE AIR!"
THUMP! SHE HIT MY HAND!!!

NOT ONLY DO I THINK SHE COULD HEAR US,
BUT I RECKON SHE COULD SEE US, TOO!
WE BELIEVED SHE'D CHOSEN US
BEFORE WE'D EVEN MADE HER BODY.
BECAUSE OUR BIRTHDAY IS NOT
THE BEGINNING OF OUR LIFE,
IT'S JUST THE DAY WE CAME TO EARTH:
OUR "EARTHDAY".

SO HER SPIRIT, BEING ALIVE BEFORE HER BODY,
CHOSE US TO BE HER EARTH-PARENTS
AND, WHILE HER BODY WAS FORMING AND GROWING,
HER SPIRIT WAS ABLE TO COME 'N' GO FROM HER BODY.
IN FACT, *THIS MAY HAVE BEEN CAUGHT ON CAMERA!*
LOOK AGAIN AT THE ULTRASOUND IMAGE FROM P. 32.
DO YOU SEE WHAT I SEE? IS THAT AN IMAGE
OF HER SPIRIT, LOOKING HER BODY IN THE FACE!?!

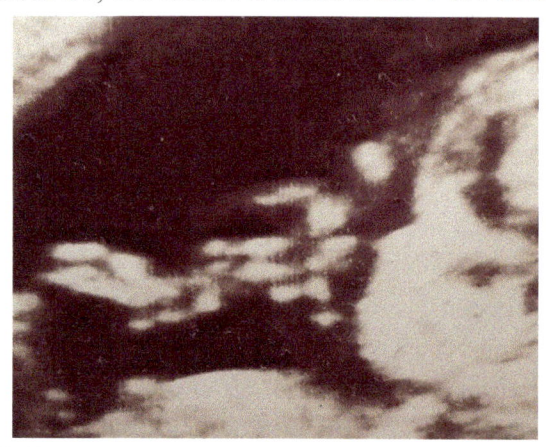

THIS WASN'T IN ANY OF THE 7 OTHER PHOTOS.

I *HAVE* ASKED MYSELF,
"IF WE CHOOSE OUR LIVES,
WHY ON EARTH WOULD A SPIRIT CHOOSE A BODY
THAT IT KNOWS WON'T BE WITH US LONG!?!"

I BELIEVE THE ANSWER IS THIS...
...*THEY WANTED TO BE <u>WITH US</u>
MORE THAN THEY WANTED TO BE BORN!*

YOU SEE, THEY CHOSE US TO BE THEIR PARENTS
OUT OF ALL THE BILLIONS OF PEOPLE...
...NOT FOR THE LIFE THEY SAW...
...BUT TO BE OUR CHILDREN FOREVERMORE!
THEY KNEW THAT OUR SPIRITS WOULD BE TOGETHER
FOR ETERNITY IN THE SPIRIT REALM!
THEY LOVE US MORE THAN THEIR PHYSICAL LIFE!

I'M STILL A DAD!
NOTHING WILL *EVER* CHANGE THAT!
I HAVE A DAUGHTER-IN-SPIRIT!
HER NAME MEANS, "SPIRIT (KA) OF THE SUN (RA)"!
I LOVE HER....AND SHE LOVES ME....THIS *I KNOW.*
"DEATH" CANNOT QUENCH LOVE'S FIRE,
NOR CAN IT DIM LIFE'S LIGHT!

KaRa HAS BEEN GIVING MANY SIGNS OF HER OWN,
NEARLY ALWAYS USING A SEAGUL AS HER SYMBOL.
IT BEGAN DURING THE LEAD UP TO FATHER'S DAY,
JUST WEEKS AFTER THE FIRE.
I WAS GETTING REALLY SAD,
SEEING FATHER'S DAY THINGS EVERYWHERE.

FATHER'S DAY WAS DUE, JUNE 19TH.
KaRa'S DUE DAY....WAS THE 20TH.

I FELT SO LOW AND BEREFT.
I PICKED UP A NEWSPAPER
TO TRY TO DISTRACT MYSELF.
I BEGAN TO BLANKLY PAGE THROUGH IT.
THEN A NAME IN A HEADLINE STOOD OUT TO ME:

"KARA"

I FROZE FOR A MOMENT, IN DISBELIEF.

SUCH AN UNUSUAL NAME,
WITH AN EVEN MORE UNUSUAL SPELLING,
STARTING WITH A "K" INSTEAD OF A "C".

APPARENTLY, KARA,
A LITTLE GIRL OF 4 YEARS,
HAD BEEN ATTACKED BY SEAGULLS.

I WAS SO PLEASED...
...NOT 'COS A CHILD GOT BIRD-BULLIED, SILLY...
...BUT, TO GET A LITTLE SIGN FROM HER,
JUST WHEN I WAS REALLY MISSING HER.

SOME MORE DAYS WENT BY.
FATHER'S DAY WAS THE NEXT DAY OR SO.
I HAD SPIRALLED DOWNWARDS AGAIN AND
JUST SAT QUIETLY WITH STREAMING EYES.
AGAIN, I PICKED UP A PAPER FOR DISTRACTION...

...I BEGAN TO PAGE THROUGH IT ROUGHLY,
WHEN SOMETHING COUGHT MY EYE...
...A PICTURE OF A SEAGUL!

I READ THE STORY EAGERLY,
TO SEE IF THERE WERE ANY SIGNIFICANT NAMES.
SEAGULLS WERE ON THE RAMPAGE AGAIN,
THIS TIME ATTACKING A GROWN MAN...
...WHOSE LAST NAME WAS...
...**"STEWART"**!

OKAY, IT'S NOT THE SAME SPELLING AS MINE,
BUT I'M NOT GONNA PULL UP MY
8-MONTHS-GESTATED BABY
ON A SPELLING MISTAKE!
SHE'S A GENIUS!

I WROTE ABOUT THIS IN "THE COMFORTER",
BUT WHAT WASN'T INCLUDED IN THERE,
WAS THE FINAL PART TO THIS STORY,
BECAUSE IT HADN'T HAPPENED
BEFORE I PRINTED THE BOOK,
SO HERE'S THE MISSING PIECE:

SINCE THE FIRE, I HAD ONLY ONCE
ATTEMPTED TO CLEAN THE FLAT
AND EVERYTHING IN IT.
IT WASN'T UNTIL 2018,
THAT I WAS STRONG ENOUGH
- PHYSICALLY AND MENTALLY -
TO PROPERLY DECORATE.

I HAD BEEN BUSY PAINTING THE KITCHEN
AND OLD NEWSPAPERS WERE EVERYWHERE.
I STOPPED TO HAVE SOME LUNCH.
I WENT TO CLEAN MY HANDS TO EAT,
BUT I'D COVERED THE SINK WITH PAPER.

I SLID THE PAGES TO ONE SIDE
AND WAS SUDDENLY CONFRONTED
WITH AN IMAGE OF A SQUAWKING SEAGULL!
I IMMEDIATELY BEGAN FRANTICALLY READING,
HOPING TO FIND A PERSON'S NAME RELEVANT...
...BUT NOTHING.
I COULDN'T BELIEVE IT.
THERE *HAD* TO BE A SIGN HERE!
I READ AND RE-READ IT, DESPERATELY.
NO ONE'S NAME HAD ANY CONNECTION WITH US.

THEN I NOTICED THE NAME OF THE PLACE
WHERE THE SEAGULLS HAD NOW BEEN
MAKING A NUISANCE OF THEMSELVES...
...CARBIS BAY!!!

THIS WAS INDEED SIGNIFICANT, BECAUSE,
WHILE GROWING UP IN SOUTH AFRICA,
THE WHITE PEOPLE ALWAYS STRUGGLED
TO READ/SAY KHABI'S NAME CORRECTLY,
SO THEY ALWAYS PRONOUNCED IT,
"CARBEE" INSTEAD OF, "CABBY".

BECAUSE OF THIS, KHABI USED "CARBEE"
MOST OF THE TIME, EVEN ON FACEBOOK!

AGAIN, NOT PERFECT SPELLING,
BUT WHAT MORE DO YOU WANT FROM
A BABY THAT HADN'T EVEN BEEN BORN!
SHE'S INCREDIBLE! I'M *SO* PROUD OF HER!
WAS THIS DEFINATELY A SIGN FROM HER!?!
WELL...*THAT* DAY...*WAS* FATHER'S DAY!
BLESS YOU BABY K! BANG ON TIME!
I COULD GO ON AND ON, BUT,
LET ME END ON A MOVING MUSICAL NOTE!

WHEN I FINALLY I MUSTERED THE STRENGTH
TO MAKE SOME ENQUIRIES ABOUT HEADSTONES,
I CALLED THE FUNERAL HOME.
THE LADY I SPOKE TO WAS VERY NICE AND HELPFUL.
AT THE END OF THE CALL SHE TOLD ME,
IF I HAD ANY MORE QUESTIONS TO CALL HER...
...AND THAT HER NAME WAS KARA!
"CARLA?", I ASKED, NOT QUITE BELIEVING MY EARS.

"NO! *KARA!* LIKE THE SONG, 'KARA, KARA'!"

I'D NEVER HEARD OF IT, SO OF COURSE, I GOOGLED IT.
IT'S BY <u>*NEW WORLD*</u> AND HAS SOME POIGNANT LYRICS:
"YOU CAN STILL FEEL HIS HAND
AS YOU HEARD HIM SAY
IN THE WORDS OF THE ISLANDS
I'LL RETURN ONE DAY.
KARA, KARA, KARA KIMBIAY,
THE STARS WILL GUIDE ME ON MY WAY
"....KARA, KARA WAIT FOR ME
WHEN I RETURN ACCROSS THE SEA
KARA, KARA, I'LL BE BACK TO STAY."

CHAPTER 12...CONCLUSIONS

SO WHAT DOES ALL THIS TELL US!?!
IT SAYS THAT **WHEN SOMEONE DIES,
IT IS ONLY THE BODY THAT HAS DIED**,
WHILE A PART THEM REMAINS
ALIVE AND UNTOUCHED
BY THE EVENTS OF THIS WORLD.

WHAT PART OF THEM SURVIVES THE BODY?
WELL...RIGHT NOW, THINK OF A RED BALLOON.
WHERE IS THAT BALLOON?
IT'S IN YOUR MIND, SURE, BUT
WHERE IS THAT IMAGE BEING DISPLAYED
FOR YOU TO SEE IT IN YOUR MIND'S EYE?

THERE IS NO SCREEN IN YOUR HEAD
WITH THE PICTURE OF A RED BALLOON ON IT.
IT IS SOMEWHERE ELSE.

WHERE IS YOUR MIND?
IS IT IN YOUR BRAIN? NO.
MIND, BY ITS VERY NATURE,
IS NOT A PHYSICAL OBJECT.

BECAUSE MIND IS NOT PHYSICAL,
IT CANNOT BE TOUCHED
AND WHAT CANNOT BE TOUCHED
CANNOT BE DESTROYED.
CAN YOU BREAK THE AIR?
NO....YOU CAN ONLY BREAK WIND! LOL!

SERIOUSLY THOUGH,
SOMETHING THAT IS NOT PRESENT
IN THIS PHYSICAL WORLD
SHALL FOREVER BE BEYOND ITS REACH.

I HAD A DREAM ONCE,
WHERE I WAS FALLING FROM A BUILDING.
I KNEW I WAS GONNA HIT THE GROUND, BUT
THERE WAS ABSOLUTELY NOTHING I COULD DO
TO PREVENT THE INEVITABLE.

I WAS LOOKING UP AT THE SKY AS I FELL...THEN...
...I FELT A SENSATION AT THE BACK OF MY HEAD
AND THE NEXT THING I REMEMBER,
I'M LOOKING AT THE BUILDING
THAT I HAD JUST FALLEN FROM.

BUT, I WASN'T LOOKING AT IT FROM THE GROUND,
I HAD THE AWARENESS OF BEING
ALMOST HALFWAY UP THE BUILDING
AND I COULDN'T FEEL MY WEIGHT
OR ANYTHING PHYSICAL.

HOWEVER,
*I WAS ALSO AWARE
THAT I WAS STILL THINKING TO MYSELF...
...EVEN THOUGH I'D JUST DIED!*
AND IN THAT MOMENT IT DAWNED ON ME
THAT **IT IS OUR THOUGHTS THAT SURVIVE DEATH!**
I THOUGHT TO MYSELF AS I LOOKED AT THE BUILDING,
"I MUST HAVE JUST DIED....BUT I'M STILL THINKING..
...I'M STILL ME!"

SO THERE'S A PART OF A PERSON
THAT DOES NOT DIE...
...THE PERSONALITY!

IT'S HARD TO COMPREHEND, I KNOW,
BUT LOOK AT IT LIKE THIS:

LET'S GO BACK TO THE FACT THAT WE DREAM,
BECAUSE, NIGHT AFTER NIGHT,
A MESSAGE IS BEING DESPERATELY CONVEYED
BUT WE NEVER REALIZE WHAT IT'S SAYING!

WE DREAM WHILE WE SLEEP.
TO BE MORE PRECISE,
OUR MIND DREAMS BECAUSE OUR BODY IS ASLEEP.
WHAT DOES THIS IMPLY!?!

IT IS TRYING TO REMIND US
THAT THERE IS A PLACE WE CAN GO
THAT IS NOT A PHYSICAL PLACE.
IT ALSO SAYING THAT
THERE IS A PART OF US THAT CAN FUNCTION
WITHOUT THE BODY.

THE MIND, OR CONSCIOUSNESS, OR SOUL,
DOES NOT REQUIRE THE BODY
TO LIVE AND EXPRESS,
EXPERIENCE AND REMEMBER.
THE MIND WILL GO ON
LIVING, LOVING AND LEARNING.
LIFE CARRIES ON. *LITERALLY!*

CONSIDER THE RED BALLOON
THAT YOU PICTURED IN YOUR MIND.
COULD ANYONE BURST IT? NO.
IF SOMEONE SMASHES YOUR HEAD IN,
WILL IT BURST THE BALLOON? NO.

NOW...
...INSTEAD OF THINKING OF THE BALLOON,
PICTURE YOURSELF.
PICTURE YOURSELF CLEARLY.
PICTURE YOURSELF HEALTHY AND HAPPY.

THAT VERSION OF YOU...
...LIKE THE BALLOON...
...CAN NEVER BE DESTROYED.
THE PHYSICAL YOU CAN BE KILLED,
BUT WHAT WE HAVE SEEN PROOF OF
IN THE PRECEDING PAGES, IS THAT
THE MENTAL YOU WOULDN'T DIE WITH THE BODY.

THE ONES WE MISS SO DEARLY...
...THEY'RE *SAFE*, THEY'RE *FREE*, THEY'RE *HAPPY*.
THEY DIDN'T ACTUALLY DIE!

THERE'S A BEAUTIFUL POEM,
BY ELIZABETH FRYE,
THE TITLE OF WHICH IS THE FIRST LINE I QUOTE:
"DO NOT STAND AT MY GRAVE AND WEEP;
I AM NOT THERE. I DO NOT SLEEP.
"....DO NOT STAND AT MY GRAVE AND CRY;
I AM NOT THERE. I DID NOT DIE."

WHERE ARE THEY THEN?
THEY ARE WITH US ALWAYS.
I READ A BOOK ONCE, THAT SAID,
"THEY ARE NEARER THAN HANDS AND FEET"!
WHERE IS THE NON-MATERIAL WORLD?
IT MUST BE **JUST BEHIND THE MATERIAL WORLD.**
IT MUST BE **HERE, WITH US,**
RATHER THAN SOMEWHERE FAR AWAY,
OTHERWISE WE WOULD NOT BE ABLE
TO FEEL THEIR PRESENCE,
OR RECEIVE HEALING,
LIKE I DID.

THEY MAY BE **GONE FROM OUR SIGHT...**
...BUT THEY ARE **NOT** GONE **FROM OUR SIDE**,
THEY SIMPLY STAND IN A DIFFERENT LIGHT,
JUST BEYOND THE SCOPE OF OUR EYESIGHT.

OUR EYES ONLY SEE A SMALL PERCENTAGE,
UNDER 1%, OF THE FULL LIGHT SPECTRUM,
SO JUST BECAUSE WE CAN'T SEE SOMETHING,
IT DOESN'T MEAN IT ISN'T THERE.

SO WHAT ABOUT HEAVEN AND HELL!?!

I BELIEVE THESE ARE MENTAL STATES
RATHER THAN PLACES.
TO EXPLAIN,
LET US QUICKLY LOOK AT AN N.D.E.
(NEAR DEATH EXPERIENCE)
THAT I READ ABOUT.

A MAN HAD BEEN IN HOSPITAL,
WHEN HIS BODY DIED.
THE DOCTORS NEVER GAVE UP
AND AFTER QUITE SOME TIME,
THEY MANAGED TO RESUSCITATE HIM.

WHILE HIS BODY HAD LAIN THERE, DEAD,
HE HAD BEEN HAVING AN EXPERIENCE
OF GOING TO A PLACE FILLED WITH LIGHT,
WHERE PEOPLE WERE THERE TO GREET HIM.
HE WAS THEN SHOWN A LIFE REVIEW.
HE WAS SHOWN ALL HIS DEEDS AND ACTIONS.
HE SAW HIMSELF BEING MEAN TO HIS LITTLE SISTER
WHEN THEY WERE KIDS.

HE SAID HE FELT THE PAIN HE MADE HER FEEL.
HE SAID IT WAS THE WORST PAIN HE'D EVER KNOWN,
FOR HE WAS FEELING THE PAIN HE CAUSED,
BUT IT WAS MULTIPLIED.

THAT IS THE PUNISHMENT.
YOU FEEL ALL PAIN YOU CAUSED
A HUNDRED-FOLD, BECAUSE GUILT IS ACIDIC.
THAT IS THE BURNING SULPHUR OF HELL.

IF ALL YOU'VE DONE IS CAUSE PEOPLE PAIN,
THEN, BY YOUR OWN DOING,
THERE IN HELL, YOU SHALL REMAIN.
BUT IF YOU'VE SPREAD JOY AND LIGHT,
THAT, TOO, SHALL BE MAGNIFIED,
WHICH WILL BE YOUR HEAVENLY GAIN.

CHAPTER 13...A MESSAGE TO THE BEREAVED

LIFE REALLY *IS* UN-ENDING.
ETERNAL LIFE IS A FACT OF NATURE,
NOT DEPENDANT ON *ANYTHING*.
**IT IS AUTOMATIC
AND IT'S FOR EVERYONE.**

HOW IT IS FOR YOU, ON THE OTHER SIDE,
DEPENDS ON HOW YOU'VE BEHAVED ON THIS SIDE.

IN VIEW OF THIS, I HAVE TWO MESSAGES.
THE FIRST IS TO THE FAMILY AND FRIENDS
OF THE INNOCENTS LOST:

**(Their name/s here)..
IS/ARE ALIVE AND WELL IN THE SPIRIT REALM.**

**THEIR MIND IS NO LONGER CONFINED
TO THEIR BODY.
THEY ARE WITH YOU
WHENEVER YOU WANT THEM TO BE.**

THEY WONT MISS A THING...
...YOUR BIRTHDAY, YOUR WEDDING,
YOUR GRADUATION, YOUR ACHIEVEMENTS,
THE BIRTH OF YOUR CHILDREN, ETC...
THEY WILL SEE IT ALL...
...EVEN IF THEY WERE BLIND,
FOR NOW THEY SEE EVEN MORE THAN WE CAN!

FOR ME, R.I.P. STANDS FOR
"RESTORED IN PERFECTION",
BECAUSE WHEN WE RETURN TO SPIRIT,
WE LEAVE THE BODY BEHIND, ALONG WITH
ALL ITS LIMITATIONS, DAMAGE OR DISABILITY!
THE SPIRIT NEVER SUFFERS WHAT THE BODY DOES.
THE BAD THINGS THAT HAPPEN IN OUR LIVES,
HAPPEN *AROUND* US , BUT NOT *TO* US.

WE ARE NOT OUR BODY,
WE RESIDE *IN* OUR BODY
WHILST LIVING ON EARTH.
WE ARE INFINITE BEINGS,
ETERNAL MINDS,
EXPERIENCING A MULTITUDE
OF EXPRSSSIONS OF LIFE AND REALITY.

IT MATTERS NOT SO MUCH
WHAT INJUSTICES AND PAINS BEFALL US,
AS *HOW WE BEHAVE*
IN RESPONSE TO THOSE THINGS, DOES.
THE TEST OF LIFE,
IS TO SEE IF WE REMAIN GOOD PEOPLE...
...EVEN IF THE WORLD SEEMS BAD;
TO REMAIN RIGHTEOUS,
EVEN WHEN SUCCESS CAN BE
EASILY ATTAINED UNRIGHTEOUSLY;
TO KEEP GOING,
EVEN IF WE FEEL LIKE GIVING UP.

TO RISE ABOVE THE PAIN, REMEMBER...

...THE MIND NEVER DIES,
FOR WHAT IS NOT PHYSICAL
CANNOT EVER BE DESTROYED.

"I THINK THEREFORE I AM", MEANS
AS LONG AS YOU'RE THINKING, YOU'RE ALIVE.

HERE IS AN EQUATION I CAME UP WITH TO EXPRESS
THE INCONSEQUENCE OF PHYSICAL DEATH UPON LIFE:

MIND = LIFE.

ALSO,
MIND + BODY = LIFE,

ALTHOUGH,
LIFE (BODY + MIND) − MIND = BODY

AND
BODY (LIFE − MIND) = DEATH.

HOWEVER,
LIFE (BODY + MIND) − BODY = MIND

AND
MIND (LIFE − BODY) = LIFE,

SO,
LIFE = MIND + / − BODY.

DEATH IS ONLY EXPERIENCED BY THE BODY, SO
YOU WILL SEE AND HOLD THEM AGAIN SOME DAY,
I PROMISE!

I CAN PROMISE YOU THAT,
BECAUSE I ALREADY HAVE
AND I DIDN'T NEED A NEAR-DEATH-EXPERIENCE
FOR IT TO TAKE PLACE.
**IT HAPPENS IN YOUR SLEEP,
WHETHER YOU REMEMBER, OR NOT!**
AND IT CAN BE BROUGHT ON
BY VIVIDLY PICTURING THEM
JUST BEFORE YOU SLEEP.

THEY LOVE YOU SO MUCH.
EVEN IF THEY DIDN'T KNOW
HOW TO BE LOVING IN LIFE,
THEY DID LOVE YOU REALLY
AND **THEY LOVE YOU STILL**, NOW.

BECAUSE THEY LOVE YOU,
IT BREAKS THEIR HEART TO SEE YOU HURTING, BUT
THEY UNDERSTAND AND THEY ARE WITH YOU NOW,
WRAPPING YOU IN WINGS OF LOVE.

TRY TO BE COMFORTED,
KNOWING ALL IS NOT WHAT IT SEEMS
IN THIS WORLD OF ILLUSIONS.
TRY, ALSO, NOT TO FOCUS ON HOW THEY PASSED,
FOR THAT DAY'S NOT SOMETHING THEY DWELL ON.
THEY'VE MOVED ON FROM THAT DAY, *AS MUST WE.*

THE AWFUL THING THAT HAPPENED,
MAY HAVE HAPPENED TO SET THEM FREE!
I'M NOT JUSTIFYING THE MURDER, *NEVER!*
I BELIEVE LIFE IS SO PRECIOUS,
THAT EVEN AN ANIMALS LIFE
SHOULD NOT BE TAKEN.
I'M JUST TRYING TO FIND
SOME SENSE IN THE SENSELESS.

KHABI HAD A VERY PAINFUL CHILDHOOD,
EXPERIENCED HIGH-JACKING ON THE SCHOOL BUS,
VERY STRICT CHURCH AND HELLISH BOARDING SCHOOL,
WHERE MANY CHILDREN TURNED TO GLUE FOR ESCAPE!
SOME EVEN CONSIDERED SUICIDE.
THINGS HAD GOTTEN SO BAD FOR HER,
SHE TOLD ME THERE WAS A TIME
WHEN SHE'D COMPLETELY CEASED TO SPEAK..
WHAT KIND OF TRAUMA DOES THAT TO A CHILD!!!???

SHE STRUGGLED WITH DEPRESSION
ON AND OFF, THE WHOLE TIME I KNEW HER.
YES, SHE HAD HAPPY TIMES,
BUT SHE NEVER SEEMED TO BE ABLE TO STAY HAPPY.
SOMETHING INESCAPSABLE WAS TROUBLING HER.
MAYBE SHE WAS TAKEN FROM US WITH COMPASSION,
LIKE A MOTHER LOVINGLY HUSHING HER BABY AS SHE
STEALS IT AWAY FROM THE HORRORS ALL ABOUT.
WE ARE STILL HERE, STILL FIGHTING ON,
BECAUSE, THANKFULLY,
WHAT WE'VE BEEN THROUGH
HASN'T *COMPLETELY* BROKEN US.
WE WILL BE OK. WE WERE KEPT SAFE FOR A REASON.

KEEP THIS TRUTH
AT THE FOREFRONT OF YOUR MIND:

THOSE WHO ARE
RESTORED IN PERFECTION
DO NOT NEED TO
REST IN PEACE!

REST IS WHAT A BODY NEEDS, BUT
NO MUSCLES – NO TIREDNESS!
JUST LIFE AND ENERGY.
THE ENERGY OF ETERNAL LIFE IS LOVE.
THE MORE YOU LOVE, THE MORE YOU LIVE
(IF THERE'S NO LOVE IN YOUR HEART,
YOU'RE DEAD ALREADY!).

THEY ARE SOMEWHERE CLOSER THAN WE REALIZE.
THEY CAN HEAR AND SEE US.

IT'S NEVER TOO LATE TO SAY THE THINGS
YOU WISH YOU SAID TO THEM.
IT'S NOT TOO LATE TO SHOW THEM THE THINGS
YOU NEVER GOT TO SHOW THEM
WHILST THEY WHERE VISIBLE IN THE PHYICAL REALM.
PICTURE THEM NEXT TO YOU,
HUGGING YOU OR HOLDING YOUR HAND...
...AND THEY PROBABLY ARE!

NOW, LET ME SHARE WITH YOU ONE MORE SIGN,
THAT VIVIDLY AND TOUCHINGLY SHOWS US THAT

**DEATH HASN'T GOT THE POWER
TO END LOVE AND COMPANIONSHIP:**
BOTH KHABI AND I LOVE OUR REGGAE MUSIC,
OFTEN ATTENDING DANCES, SOMETIMES DJ'ING.
THAT BEING SAID, HOWEVER,
I COULDN'T ATTEND ANY DANCES FOR SOME TIME
AFTER KHABI WAS RESTORED IN PERFECTION,
AS I HAD VERY LITTLE PHYSICAL STRENGTH
TO CYCLE THERE, DANCE AND CYCLE BACK,
I COULDN'T FACE SEEING PEOPLE AND
I JUST FELT MISERABLE ALL THE TIME.
WHEN SHE WAS ALIVE-IN-FLESH,
I HATED GOING TO DANCES WITHOUT HER.
EVERYTHING WAS BETTER IF SHE WAS THERE.

US AT RODDIE'S DANCE AT THE BOROUGH.

BUT, AS SOON AS I COULD,
I WENT TO A ROOTS REGGAE DANCE.
IT WAS BEING HELD AT THE BOROUGH PUB,
ON SOUTHEND SEAFRONT,
RIGHT ACROSS THE ROAD FROM THE BEACH.
IT WAS THE VENUE I WAS AT THE NIGHT OF THE FIRE.

AT SOME POINT DURING THE DANCE,
AROUND HALF TEN / ELEVEN PM,
I LITERALLY FELT URGED
TO STEP OUTSIDE THE DANCE
AND GO AND TAKE A BREATHER
BY THE WATERS' EDGE,
JUST AS ME AND KHABI USED TO.

I WENT AND SAT EXACTLY WHERE WE USED TO SIT.
I SAT LOOKING OUT ACROSS THE WATER,
WHICH WAS GENTLY RIPPLING IN THE MOONLIGHT.

THEN, IN THE DISTANCE,
I COULD SEE SOMETHING ON THE WATER.

I COULDN'T QUITE MAKE IT OUT,
BUT IT WAS COMING CLOSER.

THEN THERE IT WAS...A BEAUTIFUL SWAN!

IT SILENTLY MADE ITS WAY OVER TO ME
AND STOPPED AND JUST SAT LOOKING AT ME
FROM ABOUT 20 FEET AWAY!

TO SEE A SWAN ON SEA-WATER
IN ITSELF WAS STRANGE, BECAUSE
THEY USUALLY ONLY SETTLE ON FRESH WATER.
BUT TO SEE ONE ALONE IS VERY UNUSUAL,
AS THEY ARE KNOWN TO MATE FOR LIFE.

I KNEW IT REPRESENTED KHABI.
I KNEW SHE WAS TELLING ME
THAT SHE'S WITH ME STILL.

I SPENT A GOOD TEN MINUTES THERE.
THE SWAN JUST FLOATED ON THE SPOT,
DOING NOTHING, JUST LOOKING AT ME.
IT WAS NOT GOING TO LEAVE ME!

THEN I GOT DISTRACTED BY THE FULL-MOON,
AS IT WAS ENCIRCLED BY A SMALL RAINBOW RING.

I DON'T KNOW HOW,
BUT THIS MADE ME FORGET ABOUT THE SWAN
AND I BEGAN TO WALK BACK TO THE DANCE.

BUT I DID SUDDENLY REMEMBER THE SWAN
AND LOOKED BACK....IT WAS STILL THERE,
SITTING IN THE MOONLIGHT, WATCHING ME!

I KNEW I'D BEEN ON A SPIRITUAL DATE THAT NIGHT.
KHABI IS MY WIFE...FROM LIFE TO LIFE.
SHE KNEW THAT. I KNEW THAT. I'D TOLD HER THAT.

WE'LL BE TOGETHER AGAIN,
WHEN I COME HOME, BABE! X

SO TOO, WILL YOU BE REUNITED
WITH THE ONES YOU MISS SO DEARLY!
YOU WILL HOLD THEM AGAIN.
FEEL THEIR EMBRACE. HEAR THEIR VOICE.
SMELL THEIR SCENT. FEEL THEIR VIBE.

MOURNING WILL HAVE BROKEN.

**LIKE WHEN A MOTHER GIVES BIRTH,
THE AGONY OF THE LABOUR IS GONE
ONCE SHE LOOKS INTO THE EYES
OF THE ONE SHE HAS LONGED TO SEE.**

**NO MATTER HOW MANY HOURS
THE LABOUR LASTED,
SEEING THAT FACE
TAKES THE PAIN AWAY.
SO TOO, WILL THE PAIN
OF MISSING OUR LOVED ONES,
WHOM WE HAVE BEEN LONGING
TO ONCE AGAIN GAZE IN THE EYES OF, END,
<u>ONCE WE SEE THEIR FACES SMILING BACK AT US.</u>**

<u>THEN *WE WILL WISH WE HADN'T WASTED SO MUCH TIME* OF OUR PRECIOUS LIVES IN PAIN, *LONGING FOR THE INEVITABLE.*</u>

WE HAVEN'T BEEN TAKEN YET BECAUSE
WE ARE MEANT TO LIVE AND LOVE SOME MORE.

**THEY SURVIVED THEIR MURDER...
...AND SO MUST WE!!!**

TRY NOT TO THINK ABOUT THE DAY, OR THE WAY,
THEY WERE RETURNED TO SPIRIT.
THEY DON'T!

THEY HAVE MOVED ON FROM THAT DAY.
SO SHOULD WE TRY OUR BEST TO.

MOST PSYCHIC CONTACT WITH SPIRITS
INFORMS US THAT THEY DON'T EVEN REMEMBER
THE CIRCUMSTANCES OF THEIR CROSSING OVER.
WHAT HAPPENED, HAPPENED FOR A REASON...
...*FOR THEM, NOT FOR US.*
THE PEOPLE I KNOW
THAT HAVE PASSED EARLY OR SUDDENLY
SEEMED TO HAVE HAD A REASON OR NEED
TO BE BACK IN THE SANCTUARY OF LIGHT.

WE, TOO, HAVE BEEN/ARE GOING THROUGH
SOME NIGHTMARISH SCENARIOS,
BUT WE ARE STILL HERE
BECAUSE WE HAVE TO WIN THE BATTLE,
IF NOT FOR OURSELVES,
BUT FOR THOSE WHO STAND BY US IN SPIRIT,
WHO ARE URGING US ON TO LIVE
AND BE HAPPY AND SUCCESSFUL.

THEY ARE DESPERATE TO SEE US BE OK,
SO, **FOR THEM *AND* US....LET'S LIVE LIFE
WITH ZEST, APPRECIATION AND LOVE!**
WE MAY FIND OURSELVES IN SHITUATIONS
WE NEVER DREAMT WE WOULD BE IN...

...BUT, OH, WASN'T THERE BEAUTY ALONG THE WAY!?!
WE MAY BE WALKING A PAINFUL AND SCARY PATH,
BUT THERE ARE BUTTERFLIES HERE AND THERE;
BREATH-TAKING SUNSETS AND BLANKETS OF STARS
MORE MAGNIFICENT THAN DICTION CAN DEPICT.

AND, NOW AND THEN,
WE CROSS PATHS WITH ANGELS, UNAWARES.
SUPRISES AND AWE AWAIT AROUND THE CORNER.
LOVE LIFE! DON'T GIVE UP ON YOUR HAPPINESS.
DON'T GIVE UP ON YOU. **LOVE YOU.** *LOVE YOU!*

**NOTHING IN THIS WORLD OF ILLUSION
DESERVES THE POWER TO STEAL YOUR SPARK!**
TAKE COURAGE.
YOU HAVE A LOVING ARMY RIGHT BEHIND YOU!
DARKNESS MAY HAVE STOLEN THE FLOWERS
FROM OUR SIGHT,
BUT THEY STILL PERFUME THE AIR,
EVEN THROUGH THE NIGHT.
TIME WILL CHASE AWAY THE SHADOWS
AND REAVEAL THE GLORY THAT'D BEEN HIDDEN.

THE SAME WAY WE HAVE BEEN
SUDDENLY SHOCKED WITH HORROR,
WE CAN ALSO BE SOON SURPRISED
BY SUDDEN BLESSINGS.
I HAVE RECENTLY FOUND
MY BIOLOIGICAL FATHER, ABDULLAH, AGED 63!
IT IS A WONDERFUL FEELING! *INDESCRIBABLE!*
IT HAS HAD SUCH A HUGE EFFECT ON ME!

MARCUS GARVEY
(THE JAMAICAN FOUNDER OF
THE BACK TO AFRICA MOVEMENT
AND PROPHET OF THE ETHIOPIAN KING,
RAS TAFARI) SAID,
"A PEOPLE WITHOUT KNOWLEDGE
OF THEIR HISTORY, IS LIKE
A TREE WITHOUT ROOTS."

A ROOTLESS TREE
CANNOT FLOURISH OR BEAR FRUIT.
NOW I HAVE FOUND MY ROOTS.
NOW I AM BEGINNING TO FLOURISH.
I HAVE MUCH FRUITS TO SHARE NOW.
MY FATHER MADE ME...*TWICE*.

PLUS I NOW HAVE BROTHERS, ALI AND ADEL,
A SISTER, LAYLA, AND A "STEP"-MUM, AYESHA!

THANK GOD I DIDN'T SUCCUMB
AND MISS OUT ON SUCH BLESSINGS!
ALHAMDULILLAH!

LOOK AT THAT!
LIFE IS FUNNY! LIFE IS AMAZING!
LIFE IS FULL OF SURPRISES...
...SOME GOOD, SOME BAD,
BUT ON THE WHOLE,
LIFE IS THRILLING. ENJOY IT!

IT REALLY IS LIKE A ROLLERCOASTER.

IT'S SCARY. IT HAS UPS AND DOWNS,
TWISTS AND TURNS.
SOMETIMES IT MAKES YOU FEEL SICK.
IT MAKES YOU SCREAM, IT THROWS YOU ABOUT.
YOU GET BATTERED AND BRUISED.
BUT YOU ENJOY THE RUSH.

YOU SQUEEZE THE HAND
OF THE ONE YOU'RE WITH,
OR YOU LOOK INTO EACH OTHERS EYES,
WITH MOUTHS AND EYES OPEN WIDE
WITH FEAR AND EXCITEMENT.

YOU QUEUE UP FOR AGES, QUITE LITERALLY,
BECAUSE WE DON'T AGE IN SPIRIT, WE JUST GROW,
FOR AGE IS A PHYSICAL PHENOMENA
THAT BEGINS AT BIRTH.

THE RIDE IS ALWAYS OVER TOO SOON
AND, IN SPITE OF ALL THE NEGATIVES,
YOU WANNA GO AGAIN!

SO ENJOY THE RIDE WITH ALL ITS THRILLS 'N' SPILLS!
THROW YOUR ARMS IN THE AIR WITH ABANDON!
LET GO OF FEAR. SCREAM. LAUGH. TAKE IN THE VIEW
AND APPRECIATE THIS MOMENT WE CALL LIFE.
IF YOU CAN'T BARE TO LOOK AHEAD,
JUST KEEP CLINGING ON,
SOON THE ROUGHNESS WILL EASE
AND YOU WILL BEGIN TO SMILE AGAIN.

NOW, THE SECOND MESSAGE IS....

CHAPTER 14...A MESSAGE TO A KILLER

PLEASE FORGIVE
THE DRAMATIC TITLE TO THIS CHAPTER.

I HOPE THAT THIS BOOK WILL BE USED TO NOT ONLY
COMFORT AND GUIDE FELLOW BEREAVED HEARTS,
BUT TO ALSO HELP GUIDE PEOPLE
WHO ARE THEMSELVES, OR ARE ASSOCIATED WITH,
PEOPLE WHO BEHAVE VIOLENTLY,
TO WAKE UP FROM THEIR OWN NIGHTMARE
AND LEAVE THAT LIFE BEHIND,
SAVING THEIR OWN LIVES...
...SAVING OTHERS.

BOB MARLEY SANG,
"IN EVERY MAN' CHEST, THERE BEATS A HEART."

WHERE THERE IS A HEART BEAT, THERE IS LIFE
AND WHILE THERE IS LIFE, THERE IS HOPE,
SO MY HOPE IS THAT THEY/YOU CAN READ THIS BOOK
AND REALIZE HOW URGENT IT IS
TO TURN THEIR/YOUR LIFE AROUND
OR TO TURN THEIR/YOUR BACK ON THOSE
WHO LIVE THAT LIFESTYLE.

IT'S NEVER TOO LATE TO BE FORGIVEN!
WHATEVER YOU MAY HAVE DONE IN THE PAST,
WHAT MATTERS MOST, IS WHAT YOU DO NOW AND
WHAT YOU DO IN THE FUTURE...WILL YOU CHANGE?
WILL YOU DO THE RIGHT THING?

ANOTHER GREAT REGGAE SINGER,
JOHNNIE CLARKE, SANG,
"THOSE WHO KNOWETH THE RIGHT
AND STILL DOETH THE WRONG...
...IT AH GO ROUGH ON THEM,
IT AH GO TOUGH ON THEM,
IT AH GO ROOOUUUGH, IT AH GO TOOOUUUGH,
IT AH GO ROUGH AND TOUGH INNA BABYLON!"

DO WHAT YOU KNOW TO BE GOOD AND RIGHT
OR SUFFER YOUR OWN CONDEMNATION.
WHETHER YOU GOT AWAY WITH IT OR NOT...
...*SOMEONE SAW YOU. SOMEONE CAUGHT YOU.*
SOMEONE WAS THERE WITH YOU!
YOU DIDN'T SEE THEM. YOU DIDN'T HEAR THEM.
BUT SOMEONE *WAS* THERE! *WHO????*

YOU! YOUR SOUL. YOUR SPIRIT. YOUR MIND.
WHATEVER YOU WANT TO CALL IT.
THE ETERNAL YOU WITHIN YOU,
WHO SEES THROUGH YOUR EYES,
FEELS WITH YOUR HEART
AND HEARS THROUGH YOUR EARS...
...A SILENT WITNESS TO YOUR LIFE.
WHAT DOES THAT MEAN?

IT MEANS THAT
WHEN THE DAY COMES
WHEN YOU LEAVE YOUR BODY BEHIND,
ALL THAT REMAINS...
...IS THAT WITNESS.
THAT WITNESS DOES NOT LIE.

IT CANNOT LIE. IT WOULDN'T LIE,
THROUGH A DESIRE AND COMPULSION
FOR TRUTH AND JUSTICE.

THE LIAR WAS THE EGO...
...THE ONE WHO CLAIMED IT COULD DO ANYTHING
AND NO ONE COULD STOP THEM.

THE ONE WHO COULD PRETEND THEY DIDN'T CARE
ABOUT THE PAIN THEY CAUSED.
WELL.....THE EGO DERIVED ITS POWER
AND ITS BEING FROM THE FLESH.

EGO IS A PHENOMENON
THAT ONLY CAME INTO EXISTENCE
WHEN MIND STARTED TO BECOME "CONTAINED" IN/
VERY SUBTLY CONNECTED TO
A HUMAN BODY.

SO WHEN THAT BODY DIES,
SO DOES THE EGO.
THEN YOU'RE LEFT WITH PURE SPIRIT,
RESTORED **I**N **P**ERFECTION.

THEN YOU REMEMBER/ARE REMINDED OF
ALL THE THINGS YOU DID AND EXPERIENCED
WHILE YOU HAD A BODY, HERE ON EARTH.
YOU ARE YOUR OWN WITNESS.

NO ONE WILL NEED TO JUDGE YOU...
...YOU WILL ALREADY BE JUDGING YOURSELF!

MEMBER OF THE ORIGINAL WAILERS,
BUNNY WAILER, SANG,
"WHAT YOUR HANDS DO,
IT'S YOUR OWN EYES THAT HAVE SEEN,
SO WON'T YOU JUDGE YOUR ACTIONS,
TO MAKE SURE THE RESULTS ARE CLEAN."
THE SOONER YOU STOP NEGATIVITY
THE LESS JUDGEMENT AND MORE MERCY
DO YOU HEAP UPON YOURSELF.
DON'T GIVE UP ON YOURSELF.
SAVE YOURSELF...FROM YOURSELF.

I FORGAVE THE MAN
WHO "KILLED" KHABI AND KaRa,
SIMPLY BECAUSE I UNDERSTAND MENTAL HEALTH
AND COULD SEE QUITE CLEARLY THAT
THIS MAN IS A TRUE SCHIZOPHRENIC.
TO HATE THE MAN-ON-MEDICATION
FOR THE BEHAVIOUR OF THE MAN-OFF-MEDICATION
DIDN'T MAKE SENSE TO ME.

AFTERALL, HE HAD BEEN TRYING TO GET
HIS MEDICATION BUT THE GP COULDN'T PROVIDE IT,
NOR COULD THEY FIND AN APPROPRIATE PLACE
FOR HIM TO GET IT FROM.
HE WAS UNABLE TO GET THE CORRECT MEDS
FOR SIXTEEN MONTHS, DURING WHICH,
HE VISITED HELL AND BROUGHT FIRE BACK WITH HIM.
WHEN HE LEARNED THAT KHABI HAD "DIED",
HE DROPPED TO THE FLOOR IN SHOCK AND SAID,
"I'M A BAD MAN!"

"MENTAL ILL-HEALTH" IS SO SAD,
BUT IT SHOULD NOT BE SEEN BY THE SYSTEM
AS A REASON TO TREAT A MUDERER
DIFFERENTLY FROM HOW
THEY WOULD TREAT A "SANE" MURDERER.
TO ME THAT MAKES NO SENSE.
SURELY EQUALITY IS TO EXPERIENCE
THE SAME TREATMENT AS THE MAJORITY!?!

FIRSTLY, TO TAKE AWAY
THE BASIC HUMAN EXPERIENCE
OF THE CONSEQUENCES OF ONE'S ACTIONS,
IS TO ROB HIM OF HIS HUMANITY.

I ALREADY SAID,
I NEVER WANTED LILLO TO GO TO PRISON...
...BUT I NEVER WANTED HIM TO WALK FREE AGAIN.
I.E. I WANTED HIM TO BE ACCOMPANIED EVERYWHERE,
LIKE HOW I USED TO ACCOMPANY MY CLIENTS,
TO THE SHOPS, TO THE DOCTOR, TO SEE FAMILY.
IN THE GARDEN. IN THE STREET. EVERYWHERE.

BUT SECONDLY,
SURELY *ANYONE* WHO IS CAPABLE
OF KILLING ANOTHER HUMAN BEING
IS MENTALLY UNWELL,
EITHER DUE TO SOME SEVERE TRAUMA IN LIFE,
DRUGS, ABUSE, OR SIMPLE CHEMICAL IMBALANCES
IN THE BRAIN/BODY:- ENJOYING BEING NASTY,
SURELY IS A SIGN OF UNWELLNESS!?!
I BELIEVE 24 HR CARE AND THERAPY ARE
THE SOLUTION, RATHER THAN PRISONS.

MY POINT IS I FORGAVE THE MAN I MET.
BUT WHETHER I FORGIVE HIM, OR NOT...
...EVEN WHETHER GOD FORGIVES HIM, OR NOT,
IS BY THE BY. WHAT THE *REAL* QUESTION IS...
...WILL HE BE ABLE TO FORGIVE HIMSELF,
WHEN HE FEELS THE HEAT OF THE FIRE *HE* SET!?!

NOW, THERE HAVE BEEN MANY CASES
OF NEAR DEATH EXPERIENCES (NDE'S)
WHERE A PERSON DIES FOR SOME TIME
AND IS THEN REVIVED BY MEDICS
ONLY TO DISCOVER THAT THEY HAVE
A MEMORY OF GOING TO "HEAVEN" AND
SEEING DEAD RELATIVES WAITING FOR THEM
IN A BRIGHTLY LIT PLACE, AT THE END OF A TUNNEL!

KHABI WAITING FOR ME, IN THE LIGHT!

OTHER PEOPLE WHO'VE EXPERIENCED NDE'S
TALK ABOUT HAVING A LIFE REVIEW.
THIS IS WHERE THEY ARE SHOWN HIGHLIGHTS
OF EVERYTHING THEY EVER DID IN LIFE.

REMEMBER I SPOKE OF
A MAN WHO SAW HIMSELF AS A CHILD
BEING MEAN TO HIS LITTLE SISTER!?! WELL,
THAT'S SOMETHING MANY PEOPLE MAY'VE DONE
BUT HE SAID THAT THE WAY IT FELT WAS *AWFUL*.

HE SAID IT WAS AN UNBEARABLE PAIN
THAT WAS INDESCRIBABLE
AND HE FELT TERRIBLE FOR WHAT HE'D DONE
AND JUST WANTED THE PAIN TO STOP.

HE FELT THE PAIN HE HAD CAUSED...
...ONLY IT WAS MAGNIFIED...
...BECAUSE THE GUILT CUTS DEEPER.

THAT'S THE SELF-INFLICTED PUNISHMENT
ONE CAN EXPERIENCE FOR SOMETHING
SEEMINGLY QUITE TRIVIAL.
HOW MUCH WORSE WOULD IT FEEL FOR SOMEONE
GUILTY OF BULLYING....OR WORSE!?!

LIFE IS ETERNAL. WE HAVE ESTABLISHED THIS.
WHETHER YOU BELIEVE IT, OR NOT, *IT IS* A *FACT*.
THIS MEANS THAT **THE VICTIMS ARE ALIVE...**
...AND THOSE THAT SENT THEM BACK TO SPIRIT...
...WILL HAVE TO FACE THEIR VICTIMS IN THE END!
THEY WILL HAVE TO ANSWER FOR THEIR ACTIONS.

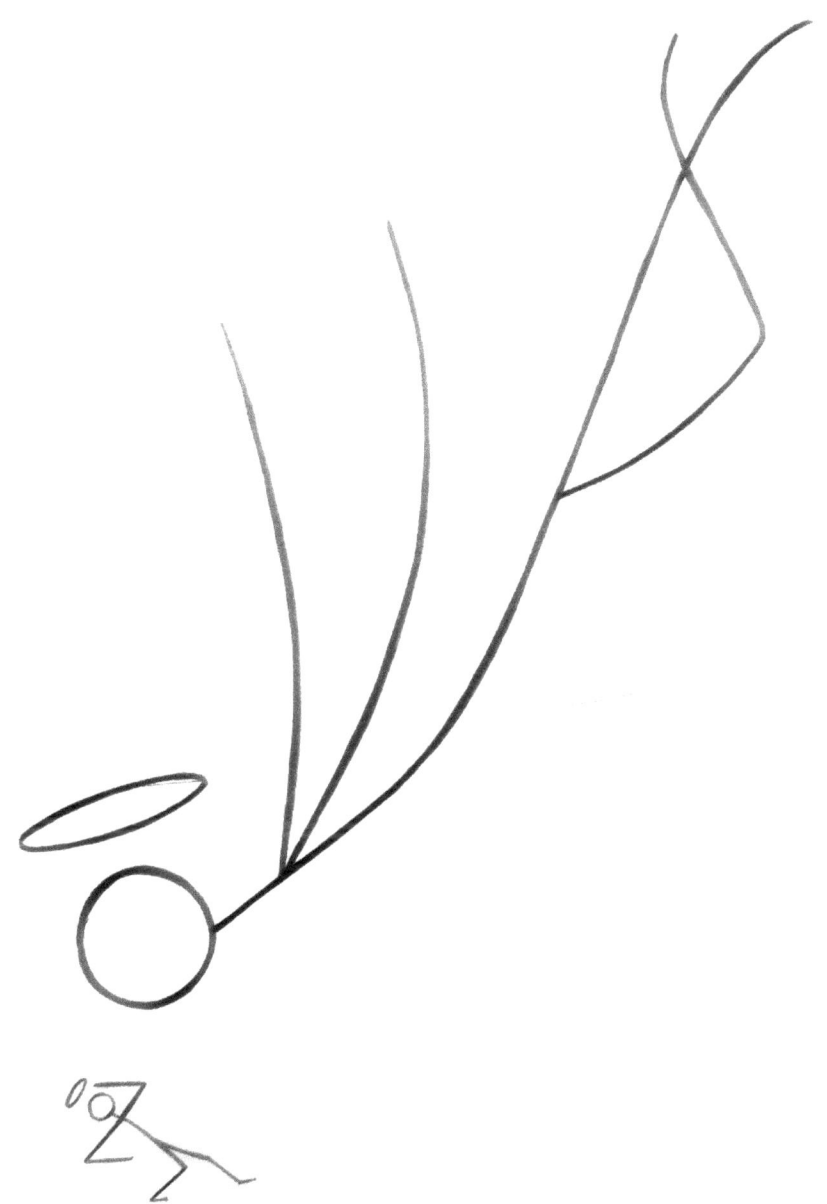

KHABI'S SPIRIT LOOMING OVER LILLO'S!
"TW0 HEAVENS CLASH".

A MURDERER ONLY KILLS A PART OF THEMSELVES,
SO REUNION
BETWEEN KILLER AND VICTIM
IS INNEVITABLE AND UNAVOIDABLE,
IN THE LIGHT,
ONLY, THIS TIME, JUSTICE WILL BE DONE.

BECAUSE LIFE IS ETERNAL,
YOU CAN'T ACTUALLY KILL ANYONE,
SO YOU CAN'T GET RID OF SOMEONE
BY KILLING THEIR FLESH.

THEY WILL ALWAYS BE WAITING FOR YOU.
YOU WILL ALWAYS HAVE TO ANSWER TO THEM.
YOU *WILL* HAVE TO FEEL THE PAIN YOU CAUSED.

NEITHER CAN YOU ESCAPE THE CONSEQUENCES
OF YOUR DEEDS BY KILLING YOU OWN FLESH.
THOSE PEOPLE THAT KILL OTHERS,
THEN KILL THEMSELVES...
...DON'T REALIZE...
...THAT BY KILLING THEMSELVES,
THEY ARE SIMPLY HASTENING
- AND WORSENING -
THEIR COMEUPPANCE.

IT'S NEVER TOO LATE TO BE GOOD, THOUGH!
THE GOD OF EVERY RELIGION
IS A MERCIFUL GOD,
IF THEY/YOU ARE SORRY ENOUGH
TO RECEIVE THAT FORGIVENESS...
...AND THEY/YOU <u>WILL</u> BE SORRY!

TRUST ME, *YOU DON'T WANT THE KARMA THAT COMES WITH CAUSING THIS KIND OF AGONY!*

LILLO ALREADY FEELS DEEPLY REMORSFUL
OVER THE PHYSICAL LIVES HE ENDED...
...AND THE PAIN HE'S CAUSED.

A COMPLETE 180!

CHAPTER 15...HEALING

ALLEGEDLY, THE FIRE WAS SET
IN AN ATTEMPT TO MAKE US MOVE OUT
BECAUSE LILLO COULDN'T STAND
HEARING ME DROP THINGS;
HEARING "ME" (THE COUNCIL) DOING DIY AND
HEARING "ME" (SOMEONE ELSE) PLAYING MUSIC.

THIS MADE ME TOO PARANOID AND ANXIOUS
TO WATCH FILMS OR LISTEN TO MUSIC
WITH ANY ENJOYABLE-YET-RESPONSIBLE VOLUME.
I HAVE BEEN TIP-TOEING AROUND MY FLAT.
I SHUDDER IF I DROP SOMETHING ON THE FLOOR.
I WORRY MY CREAKY CHAIR OR FLAPPING AIR VENT
IS WINDING SOMEONE UP ENOUGH
TO BEHAVE DANGEROUSLY TOWARD ME.

EVEN JUST PLAYING MUSIC
ON MY SMALL PORTABLE SPEAKER
DOWN BY THE BEACH OR ON MY BIKE FILLS MY HEAD
WITH THOUGHTS OF PEOPLE THINKING THINGS LIKE;
"NO WONDER THEY SET FIRE TO HIS PLACE,
HE'S ALWAYS PLAYING THAT MUSIC!"

HENCE, I'VE CEASED TO ENJOY DJ'ING IN PUBLIC.
IT'S EVEN A PROBLEM ROUND FRIENDS HOUSES!
MY BREDRIN, CLIVEY, INVITED ME ROUND
ONE TIME DURING THE SUMMER.
HE WAS T'UMPING HIS SOUND SYSTEM
AND THE WINDOWS WERE OPEN.

I WAS GETTING WORRIED PEOPLE COULD HEAR IT
AND WERE GETTING PISSED OFF.
I EVENTUALLY SAID TO HIM,
"AIN'T THAT A BIT LOUD FOR THE NEIGHBOURS!?!"

"NOOOO!", HE GOES, "THEY LOVE IT!"
"THEY TELL ME TO TURN IT UP SOMETIMES
AND WHEN I AIN'T PLAYED IT FOR WHILE,
THEY SAY WHA'S 'APPENED TO THE MUSIC!?!"

BUT THIS COULDN'T ASSUAGE MY WORRY
AND I STILL INSISTED HE TURN IT DOWN A PIECE.

ONLY SINCE ATTENDING A LENGHTY COURSE
OF COGNITIVE BEHAVIOURAL THERAPY (CBT)
HAVE I BEEN ABLE TO RELAX AND PLAY MUSIC,
ALBEIT STILL MAYBE OVERLY MINDULL OF OTHERS.

MY THERAPIST CLARIFIED, "IT WASN'T THE MUSIC
THAT CAUSED HIM TO SET THE FIRE...
...IT WAS HIS SEVERE MENTAL HEALTH ISSUES."

SHE ALSO TOLD ME,
"YOU DON'T NEED TO BE CREEPING AROUND
IN YOUR FLAT LIKE A NINJA!

"WHEN YOU NEXT WALK THE DOG,
WALK WITH EXTRA HEAVY STEPS,

"CLAIM BACK YOUR PLACE IN WORLD...
...YOU HAVE A RIGHT TO MAKE *SOME* NOISE!"

IT WAS GOOD ADVICE, BUT IT WAS A WHILE
BEFORE I FELT SAFE ENOUGH TO USE IT.
**GOING INTO THERAPY,
I WAS QUITE SKEPTICAL ABOUT
WHETHER IT WOULD BE OF ANY USE TO ME,
AS I FELT AS THOUGH I WAS BEYOND HELP**;
LIKE WHAT'D HAPPENED WAS TOO MUCH
FOR ANYONE TO BE ABLE TO HELP.

BUT I WAS ALSO DESPERATE
TO TRY ANYTHING THAT MIGHT
MAKE ME FEEL THE SLIGHTEST BIT BETTER.
I'M SO GLAD I DID IT. I CAN'T THANK HER ENOUGH!
I'M NOW GOING TO START MY OWN BUSINESS:
"ALTERNATIVE-GRIEF-GUIDANCE.CO.UK".
I ALSO PLAN TO START DOING
"MUSIC FOR MENTAL HEALTH".
I HAVE MORE CONFIDENCE NOW
AND CAN FINALLY START
MAKING PLANS FOR THE FUTURE.

BUT, IN THOSE TIMES,
MY PARANOIA WENT THROUGH THE ROOF.
I WAS OVER-ESTIMATING DANGERS.
I WAS FULL OF FEAR. IT MADE ME SO SICK.
THE WEIGHT CONTINUED FALLING OFF ME.
MY FACE WAS ALWAYS AWASH WITH SADNESS.
I COULDN'T ACCEPT SHE WASN'T COMING HOME.
I KEPT HER THINGS AS SHE LEFT THEM
AND KEPT ALL HER TOILETRIES,
JUST IN CASE SHE DID COME BACK
AND NEEDED THEM.

I THINK THE PLACE REMAINED
PRETTY MUCH UNCHANGED FOR TWO YEARS,
WITH SOME THINGS REMAINING
EXACTLY WHERE SHE'D LEFT THEM.

I MISSED/MISS HER SO MUCH.

THERE WERE TIMES WHEN
I WOULD FEEL LIKE I'M ABOUT TO CRY...
...BUT THE WAIL WOULD QUICKLY GROW LOUD
AND BECOME A LONG SCREAM,
WHICH I WOULD HAVE TO QUICKLY STIFLE
WITH EITHER MY HANDS OR A CUSHION
AS IT WOULD MAKE ME WORRIED ABOUT
ANNOYING THE NEIGHBOURS AGAIN.

I FOUND HUGGING KHABI'S DRESSING GOWN
TO BE A GREAT COMFORT
AS IT FORGED A KIND OF CONNECTION,
LIKE SHE WAS BACK IN MY ARMS.
I WOULD SPRAY HER PERFUME AND IT
INSTANTLY FELT LIKE SHE WAS WITH ME...
...ALL DRESSED UP AND READY TO GO OUT!

MANY MORNINGS,
ALTHOUGH MUCH LESS FREQUENTLY,
I WAS STILL EXPERIENCING THE NAUSEA,
THE THUMPING ON MY CHEST AND
THE FLASHING FEELING ON MY FACE,
CAUSED BY THE SHOCK OF THE EVENTS.
IT HAPPENED OVER AND OVER, UNTIL...

...I REMEMBERED, FROM MY FIRST AID TRAINING, THAT **THERE IS A POSITION TO PUT SOMEONE IN IF THEY ARE SUFFERING FROM SHOCK** AT THE SCENE OF AN ACCIDENT.

I COULDN'T REMEMBER WHAT THE POSITION WAS. I COULD ONLY REMEMBER THE RECOVERY POSITION, SO I GOOGLED IT. IT IS SIMPLY THIS:
**1. LIE DOWN FLAT ON YOUR BACK, FEET TOGETHER.
2. REST YOUR FEET ON SOMETHING THAT KEEPS THEM ABOVE THE LEVEL OF YOUR HEART. DO THIS FOR ANYTHING FROM 1-25 MINUTES.**

SO NEXT MORNING, I WOKE UP, WENT INTO SHOCK AND "THE FUN AND GAMES" BEGAN, SO I PUSHED ALL THE BED COVERS TO THE BOTTOM OF THE BED AND PROPPED MY FEET UP ON TOP.

JAH KNOW', MI NAAH LIE...
...I FELT BETTER IMMEDIATELY!
I STRONGLY RECCOMMEND YOU TRY THIS!
IT FELT AS THOUGH I'D POURED ALL THE SHOCK OUT. THE NAUSEA AND "THE HORRORS" (AS ANOTHER GOOD FRIEND PERFECTLY DESCRIBED IT WHEN HE SEPARATED FROM HIS QUEEN) ALL WASHED AWAY!

I ONLY NEEDED TO DO IT FOR A FEW MOMENTS! I DID IT THE FOLLOWING MORNING, TOO, AND THAT WAS THE LAST TIME I NEEDED TO DO IT!

APPARENTLY, SOMETHING ABOUT SENDING
ALL YOUR BLOOD BACK TO YOUR HEART
IS VERY BENFICIAL FOR MANY REASONS,
PLEASE LOOK INTO THIS.
THERE'S MORE TO IT, WHEN THEY SAY,
"PUT YOUR FEET UP"
TO RELAX!

I MUST SAY, THOUGH.
THAT I MOST LIKELY WOULDN'T HAVE BEEN ABLE
TO BE GOOGLING THESE THINGS, PUTTING MY FEET UP
AND GETTING THERAPY *AND*
BEING ABLE TO ATTEND REGULARLY,
HAD IT NOT BEEN FOR ANOTHER ANGEL
SENT TO SAVE ME!

REMEMBER BROTHER REECE!?!
HIS LOVELY AND AMAZINGLY STRONG MUM, TRACIE,
HELD A PARTY TO HONOUR HIS 30TH EARTHDAY.

IN THOSE DAYS, EVERYWHERE I WENT,
I HAD COPIES OF ME 'N' KHABI'S BOOKS IN MY BAG.

A LADY CAME UP TO ME AT THE PARTY AND SAID,
"I'VE JUST HEARD YOUR STORY
AND I WANNA BUY YOUR BOOKS!"

SO SHE BOUGHT THEM OFF ME THERE AND THEN.
IT TURNED OUT SHE BOUGHT MANY MORE
AND BASICALLY DISTRIBUTED THEM
AROUND THE WORLD!

HER NAME IS LORRAINE.
REECE WAS GOOD FRIENDS WITH HER
AND HER PARTNER, KEV, "THE CAP.",
SO NAMED AFTER THE CAPTAIN MORGAN RUM
HE AND REECE HAD MANAGED TO FINISH
COPIOUS AMOUNTS OF TOGETHER!

WE ALL BECAME REALLY GOOD FRIENDS.
LORRAINE IS INTO SPIRITUAL HEALING
AND KEV IS AN INVENTOR...
...AND A COMEDIAN...AND A MAGICIAN!
ME...I LOVE ALL THE ABOVE,
SO WE ALL GOT ON FAMOUSLY!

THEY LIFTED MY SPIRIT. THEY GAVE ME HOPE
AND THE ABILITY TO SEE A WAY FORWARD.
THE THINGS THEY HAVE DONE
FOR ME *AND* FOR MUM,
SAVED OUR LIVES AND OUR SANITY!
AMAZING PEOPLE. TRULY. THANK YOU SO MUCH!

THIS IS ANOTHER REASON WHY IT IS SO IMPORTANT
TO NEVER GIVE UP ON HOPE.
GOD/THE UNIVERSE/FATE OR
WHATEVER YOU WANT TO CALL IT,
WILL ALWAYS GIVE YOU WHAT YOU NEED.
JUST, PLEEEAAASE, DON'T GIVE UP!

IF YOU DO GIVE UP, YOU MAY NOT SEE
THE LIFE BOATS COMING YOUR WAY.
NOR WILL YOU VISIT THE BEAUTIFUL PLACES
THEY CAN TAKE YOU TO.

HAD IT NOT BEEN FOR THEIR SUPPORT,
I BELIEVE THE INQUEST WOULD HAVE
ACTUALLY PUT ME IN HOSPITAL,
EITHER FOR PHYSICAL OR
PSYCHOLOGICAL REASONS....OR BOTH.

IN FACT, ALL MY FRIENDS
SHOWED ME A LOT OF LOVE AND CARE
IN VARIOUS WAYS.

FOR A LONG TIME, I WAS STRUGGLING TO EAT.
I WENT TO VISIT MY BREDRIN, JASON, IN LONDON.

IT TOOK A LOT OUT OF ME
TO GET THERE FROM ESSEX,
AS WALKING ABOUT WAS STILL QUITE EXHAUSTING,
DUE TO THE LACK OF FOOD AND HOW DRAINED
GRIEF'S EMOTIONS MAKE YOU FEEL.

IT WAS ALMOST THREE HOURS, DOOR TO DOOR.
BUT THE LOVE AND LAUGHTER
MADE IT WORTH IT.

I TOLD JASON I WAS UNABLE TO EAT
WITHOUT FEELING NAUSEAUS,
SO HE MADE ME A SMOOTHIE
PACKED FULL OF GOODNESS.
THAT WENT DOWN, NO PROBLEM!

HE MADE A MASSIVE BOTTLE OF IT
FOR ME TO BRING HOME. BLESS UP "J"!

MY BREDRIN, JIM'S QUEEN, MEL,
MADE ME SOME LOVELY VEGAN TREATS, TOO.

SHAUN, KEETY, CLIVEY, RACHEL, DAN AND OTHERS
HAVE ALL BEEN REAL STARS. HONESTLY.
THANK YOU ALL...ESPECIALLY YOU, MUM...
FROM THE HEART OF MY HEART,
I WOULDN'T HAVE MADE IT THROUGH TO HERE
WITHOUT THE THINGS YOU DID
AND STILL DO, BIG AND SMALL.
EVERYTHING MADE A DIFFERENCE
AND IS APPRECI-LOVED!

BLESS YOU ALL!

X

FROM THE NIGHT OF THE FIRE, TO NOW, MY FRIENDS
AND FAMILY HAVE BEEN KEY TO MY HEALING.

I CAN'T STRESS ENOUGH
HOW IMPORTANT IT IS TO SPEND TIME
WITH PEOPLE YOU TRUST
AND WHO CARE FOR YOU.

NOTHING MAJOR NEED BE SAID.
NO NEED FOR EMOTIONAL OUT-POURINGS.
JUST TALKING ABOUT WHAT OTHERS ARE UP TO
TAKES YOUR MIND OFF THE THINGS
YOU SPEND YOUR TIME DWELLING ON.
YOU COULD JUST LISTEN TO MUSIC TOGETHER,
DIPPING COOKIES INTO VEGAN CHOCOLATE PUDD'!

BEING WITH CARING PEOPLE
IS THERAPEAUTIC,
BECAUSE LOVE NURTURES LIFE.

MY MUM, SANDY, AND BROTHER, LEFA,
HAVE BEEN SO SUPPORTIVE
AND STRONG FOR ME.

MUM'S BEEN INCREDIBLE, TO BE HONEST.
THERE WAS A TIME WHEN I WAS STILL STAYING
AT HER FLAT, JUST AFTER THE FIRE
AND I WAS A TOTAL WRECK AND
THE SADNESS KEPT OVERWHELMING ME.

I BROKE DOWN IN FRONT OF MUM.
SHE CAME AND HELD ME
AND TRIED TO COMFORT ME,
BUT I WAS BEYOND REACH.

I CRIED MY HEART OUT.

WITH ONE LONG WAIL,
I CRUMPLED AS MY BODY BECAME WEAK AND LIMP,
LEANING ALL MY WEIGHT ON HER SHOULDERS.

AMONGST THE DESPAIR,
I WAS CONSCIOUS OF WHAT I WAS DOING AND
I WAS FEARFUL OF PULLING HER TO THE GROUND.
BUT SHE TOOK MY WEIGHT,
LIKE I WAS LEANING ON AN IRON RAILING.
A REAL SUPERWOMAN, THAT! LOVE U MA! X

CHAPTER 16...SURVIVAL GUIDE

SO HERE IS A SUMMARY
OF THINGS TO REMEMBER
WHEN COPING WITH TRAGEDY.

YOU CAN USE IT AS A QUICK REFERENCE SECTION
THAT YOU CAN TURN TO
ANY TIME YOU NEED SOME GUIDANCE:

A.
REMEMBER THE TRUTH:
THERE IS NO END TO LIFE OR LOVE.

REMIND YOURSELF THIS
AS OFTEN AS POSSIBLE.
MAYBE WRITE IT DOWN AND
LEAVE IT WHERE YOU WILL SEE IT OFTEN.

REMEMBER THAT THERE IS A PART OF US
THAT DOESN'T NEED THE BODY
FOR IT TO EXPERIENCE AND REMEMBER DREAMS...
...THAT <u>PART OF OUR LOVED ONES</u>
<u>HAS SURVIVED AND IS</u>
<u>R</u>ESTORED <u>I</u>N PERFECTION.

B.
TRY NOT TO FOCUS ON PHYSICAL EVENTS.

WHEN WE DWELL ON HOW THEY DIED IN FLESH,
WE JUST SPIRAL DOWNWARDS, EMOTIONALLY.

WE MUST TRY TO REMEMBER THAT
THERE ARE TWO SIDES TO EVERYTHING,
INCLUDING THIS PHYSICAL WORLD
WE HAVE BEEN BORN INTO.
THE OTHER SIDE TO THIS WORLD IS
NON-MATERIAL/UN-MANIFESTED/SPIRIT/LOVELIGHT.

*WHATEVER HAPPENED TO OUR LOVED ONES,
HAPPENED IN FLESH....<u>BUT NOT IN SPIRIT.</u>*

C.
DO NOT THINK OF THEM
AS BEING IN THE COFFIN.

THAT IS JUST THEIR PERSON IN THERE.
THEIR PERSONALITY, HOWEVER,
IS FREE TO BE ANYWHERE IT WISHES,
YET <u>*THEY WILL NEVER BE FAR FROM YOU.*</u>

D.
DON'T USE PAST TENSE
TO REFER TO LOVED ONES IN SPIRIT.

<u>THEY *STILL* LIVE. THEY *STILL* LOVE.</u>

E.
KEEP TALKING TO THEM.

THEY MAY BE GONE FROM OUR SIGHT,
BUT THEY ARE NOT GONE FROM OUR SIDE, SO
<u>IT IS *NEVER* TOO LATE
TO SAY WHAT WE WANT TO SAY TO THEM.</u>

F.
DO NOT DWELL ON HOW THEY PASSED OVER.

MANY PSYCHICS REPORT THAT
THE <u>LOVED ONES IN SPIRIT
DON'T REMEMBER WHAT HAPPENED,
WHEN THEIR BODY DIED.</u>
THEY JUST REMEMBER BEING HERE WITH US
THEN SUDDENLY BEING THERE IN SPIRIT.

THEY HAVE MOVED ON FROM THAT DAY,
AS MUST WE!

G.
KEEP A "PHYSICAL" CONNECTION.

KEEP THEIR CLOTHES
OR BUY THEIR FAVOURITE SCENT.
SCENT IS POWERFUL...<u>IT CAN MAKE YOU FEEL LIKE</u>
YOU'RE BACK IN TIME AND
<u>THEY ARE STILL AROUND</u>, PHYSICALLY.

H.
LOOK AFTER YOURSELF.

EAT WELL. REST WELL.
IF EATING IS A PROBLEM,
EXPERIMENT WITH DIFFERENT FOODS
TO FIND WHAT IS EASIEST TO EAT.
I FOUND MARMITE ON TOAST, FRUIT, SMOOTHIES
AND SPICEY FOOD WERE EASIEST FOR ME TO EAT...
...PREFERABLY PREPARED BY SOMEONE ELSE!

<u>REST AS MUCH AS YOU CAN.
DON'T EXPECT TO BE ABLE TO DO AS MUCH
AS YOU DID BEFORE THE TRAGEDY.</u>

EVEN WALKING AROUND MAY BECOME LABOURED.
YOU WILL GRADUALLY GET YOUR STRENGTH BACK.
JUST TAKE TIME AND <u>BE PATIENT
WITH YOURSELF AND THE HEALING PROCESS.</u>

REMEMBER.... <u>YOUR LOVED ONES ARE WITH YOU
AND *DOING YOUR BEST FOR THEM...
...IS DOING THE BEST FOR YOURSELF!*</u>

THEY STILL LOVE YOU
AND LOVE IS BEING HAPPY
BECAUSE YOUR LOVED ONES ARE HAPPY.

**I.
KEEP IN TOUCH WITH SOMEONE/PEOPLE.**

WITH THE MUM, FAMILY AND FRIENDS
THAT I AM BLESSED WITH
I WAS ALWAYS GOING TO BE OK,
ALTHOUGH, THERE WERE MANY TIMES
WHEN I DID ACTUALLY WONDER
IF I WAS GOING TO SURVIVE THIS THING
OR NOT.

<u>PLEASE REACH OUT TO SOMEONE.</u>
YOU DON'T NEED TO TALK ABOUT THINGS
YOU DON'T WANT TO TALK ABOUT.

JUST GET OUT THE HOUSE
AND LISTEN TO SOMEONE ELSE RAMBLE.
<u>IT JUST HELPS TO CHANGE THE THOUGHT PATTERNS,</u>
EVEN IF IT IS JUST FOR A WHILE,
IT'LL GIVE YOUR MIND A BREAK.

REACH OUT TO PEOPLE.

IF FAMILY AND FRIENDS HAVE GONE QUIET,
WHETHER IT'S BECAUSE THEY HAVE HECTIC LIVES
OR THEY DON'T KNOW WHAT TO SAY TO YOU,
SEND OUT MESSAGES TO EVERYONE. LIKE,
"HEY, HOW YOU DOING, WHAT YOU UP TO?"
SOMEONE SHOULD GET BACK TO YOU.
<u>MAKE THE EFFORT TO GO SEE FRIENDS.</u>

<u>I KNOW IT'S HARD
AND YOU WORRY ABOUT
CRYING IN FRONT OF THEM
OR BRINGING THEM DOWN,
BUT GENERALLY YOU DON'T.</u>

BESIDES...SO WHAT IF YOU DO!?!
YOU HAVE EVERY RIGHT TO BE
HOWEVER YOU ARE FEELING.

<u>GENUINE FRIENDS WILL BE GLAD
TO BE THERE FOR YOU.
GIVE THEM THE CHANCE TO HELP.</u>

J.
AVOID ANGER, HATRED AND REVENGE.

THESE EMOTIONS JUST ADD TO OUR PROBLEMS.
THEY CAUSE PHYSICAL AILMENTS AND CAN LEAD TO
LOSS OF SANITY, LOSS OF FREEDOM OR LOSS OF LIFE.

ANGER IS OUR ENEMY.

I DIDN'T SPEAK OF ANGER IN THIS BOOK,
SIMPLY BECAUSE IT'S NOT ON MY MIND...
...BUT IT IS DEFINITELY THERE.

EVERYTHING WOULD WIND ME UP.
MY PATIENCE, WHICH I PRIDED MYSELF ON,
WAS GONE AND I COULDN'T HANDLE ANY STRESS.

ONE TIME, I THOUGHT I SENT AN EMAIL
REGARDING INFORMATION ABOUT THE INQUEST
TO THE WRONG PERSON. INSTANT MELT-DOWN!

SHOUTING AND SWEARING, I PICKED UP
A SMALL BAMBOO AND GLASS SIDE TABLE
AND SMASHED IT ONTO THE GROUND.
GLASS EVERYWHERE!

ANOTHER TIME,
A "HOMELESS" MAN ASKED ME FOR SOME MONEY.
I WENT INTO THE SHOP TO GET CHANGE,
BUT THEY DIDN'T HAVE ANY VEGAN FOOD,
SO I LEFT THE SHOP TO GO TO ANOTHER ONE,
EXPLAINING THIS TO THE BEGGAR AS I WENT.

BUT RATHER THAN LETTING ME GO,
HE CALLED ME OVER AND SHOWED ME A LETTER
STATING THAT £440 WAS GOING TO BE PAID TO HIM
BY THE BENEFITS SYSTEM, BY 4P.M.

"OH, THAT'S GOOD!", I RESPONDED,
"YOU'VE GOT MONEY COMING TO YOU TODAY!"

"NO, BUT I WANT MONEY *NOW*!", HE BARKED!

MY MOUTH OPENED FIRE:
"YOU'VE GOT 400 QUID COMING TO YOU
AND YOU'RE ASKING ME FOR F***ING MONEY!?!
F*** OOOOOFF! YOU'RE DOING BETTER THAN ME!
YOU'RE STANDING OUT HERE, BEGGING MONEY
AND PEOPLE THINK YOU NEED IT,
BUT YOU'RE A LIAR AND A THIEF!"
I WENT ON AND ON. HE LOOKED SO EMBARRASSED.
PEOPLE WERE COMING OUT OF SHOPS TO LOOK.
I WAS STILL RANTING AND CLAPPING AS I LEFT.

THIS WAS SO UNLIKE ME, BUT IT HAPPENED AGAIN,
WHEN I ATTENDED A MEETING WITH THE COUNCIL,
WHO WERE PLANNING TO APPLY RESTRICTORS
TO ALL FLAT WINDOWS, MEANING THAT
THE WINDOWS WOULD ONLY BE ABLE TO OPEN
APPROXIMATELY 10cm AND THE RESTRICTORS
CANNOT BE UNDONE. AT ALL!
THIS STRUCK FEAR (FEAR UPON FEAR) IN ME,
AS KHABI MOST LIKELY DIED BECAUSE SHE
COULDN'T GET THE CHILD LOCK ON THE WINDOW
UNDONE TO GET THE AIR SHE NEEDED.

MYSELF AND OTHERS PLEADED WITH THEM
NOT TO GO AHEAD WITH THIS,
BUT THE COUNCIL MEMBERS WERE
STEADFAST IN THEIR DECISION
AND CLAIMED THAT IF THERE WAS AN EMERGENCY,
"...YOU TAKE A HAMMER AND HIT THE WINDOW
IN THE CORNER, AS THAT IS ITS WEAKEST POINT"!

OH, SO THAT'S WHAT KHABI WAS MEANT TO DO!?!
IN HER FEAR AND PANIC AND DESPERATION,
POSSIBLY WITH HER EYES SHUT,
DUE TO THE ACRID SMOKE AROUND HER,
ALL THE WHILE RUNNING OUT OF AIR!

ON TOP OF IT ALL, WE WERE INFORMED
THAT WORKMEN WOULD BE COMING
TO INSTALL THE RESTRICTORS
AND IF THEY WEREN'T GRANTED ACCESS,
THEY WILL BREAK IN, DO THE WORK,
CHANGE THE LOCKS AND BILL US
FOR THE DAMAGE.
I EXPLODED AGAIN.

THEIR LACK OF UNDERSTANDING AND EMPATHY
AND THEIR REFUSAL TO ACCEPT
ANY OF OUR CONCERNS,
ESPECIALLY IN VIEW
OF WHAT HAPPENED TO KHABI AND KaRa,
WAS DISTURBING AND UPSETTING.
THE THOUGHT OF BEING CAGED IN THE FLAT,
LIKE KHABI WAS, UNABLE TO BREATHE,
FILLED ME WITH SO MUCH FEAR AND HORROR,

I HAD TO LEAVE THE MEETING AFTER MY OUTBURST,
HYPERVENTILATING AND REQUIRING ASSISTANCE
FROM AMBULANCE CREW
WHO HAPPENED TO BE THERE.

MANY OTHER TIMES,
I OVER-REACTED TO NEGATIVE THINGS
PEOPLE SAID AND DID.
I JUST WASN'T THE PERSON I WAS BEFORE.
THIS DIFFERENCE IN ME SCARED ME
AND IT WAS THIS THAT PROMPTED ME
TO SEEK THE ADVICE OF A DECENT THERAPIST.
I STRONGLY RECCOMMEND YOU DO THE SAME
IF ANY KIND OF NEGATIVE EMOTION
IS CONSUMING YOU.

MY FIRST COUNSELLOR
(WHO WAS NOT GREATLY HELPFULL)
TOLD ME "ITS UNDERSTANDABLE
FOR YOU TO BE ANGRY."
BUT I WAS NOT AWARE OF ANY ANGER AT THAT TIME.
ALL I COULD FEEL...WAS SADNESS.
THERE WERE TIMES, OF COURSE,
WHEN I WOULD START TO THINK ON THE DETAILS
OF THE TRAGEDY AND HOW IT COULD HAVE BEEN
SO DIFFERENT IF WE HADN'T BEEN IGNORED...
...BUT I SOMEHOW PUSH IT TO ONE SIDE AND
TRY NOT TO ENTERTAIN THAT LINE OF THINKING,
BECAUSE I KNOW...IF I GO THERE,
IT COULD BECOME AN ALL CONSUMING FIRE.
THERAPY AND MEDITATION (SEE BELOW)
HELPED ME TREMENDOUSLEY.

K.
MEDITATE.

MY MUM AND I STARTED GOING TO RAJA YOGA
AS THERE WERE FREE CLASSES IN TOWN.
SOME DAYS, WE DIDN'T WANT TO GO,
AS WE FELT TOO DEPRESSED TO FACE PEOPLE,
BUT...WE WOULD COME OUT FEELING
LIFTED AND REFRESHED...AND SMILING!
GOOGLE OR CHECK SHOP NOTICE BOARDS
TO SEE IF THERE'S ANY FREE/CHEAP CLASSES NEARBY.

L.
TREAT YOURSELF FOR SHOCK.

LIE ON YOUR BACK.
REST YOUR FEET ON SOMETHING THAT
KEEPS THEM ABOVE THE LEVEL OF YOUR HEART.
<u>DO THIS TO COMBAT THE EFFECTS OF THE SHOCK
OF THE TRAUMATIC EXPERIENCE.</u>
DO IT FOR A FEW SECONDS OR UP TO 25 MINUTES.

M.
AVOID ALCOHOL.

OF COURSE, YOU'RE LIKELY TO START/INCREASE
INTAKE OF ALCOHOL IN SUCH STRESSFULL TIMES.
JUST BE AWARE THAT <u>ALCOHOL *IS A DEPRESSANT!!!*</u>
IT MAY, AT THE TIME, MAKE YOU FEEL BETTER,
BUT <u>AFTER IT HAS LEFT YOUR SYSTEM,
IT LEAVES YOU FEELING *LOWER*
THAN BEFORE</u> YOU HAD THE DRINK.

UNDERSTANDABLY, WE ALL DO
WHAT WE FEEL WE HAVE TO DO TO COPE
WITH THE THINGS WE'RE CONFRONTED WITH,
BUT <u>THERE *MUST* COME A POINT
WHERE YOU START TO *LOVE YOURSELF* AGAIN.</u>

FOR YOURSELF AND
FOR THE SPIRITS WHO STILL CARE ABOUT YOU,
<u>CHERISH YOUR LIFE AND MAKE THE MOST OF IT.</u>

<u>YOU DESERVE HEALTH. YOU DESERVE HAPPINESS.</u>
PLEASE DON'T SELF DESTRUCT.
REMEMBER...YOU ARE *STILL* LOVED...
...BY PHYSICAL *AND* SPIRITUAL BEINGS.

N.
SEEK *QUALITY* PROFESSIONAL GUIDANCE.

FIND A THERAPIST WHO YOU FIND HELPFUL.
THERAPYFORYOU.CO.UK WERE GREAT FOR ME.
IT WASN'T HOW I EXPECTED IT TO BE.
<u>THE FIRST SESSION IS THE WORST,
BECAUSE YOU HAVE TO TELL THEM
EVERYTHING THAT YOU'VE BEEN THROUGH</u>
SO THAT THEY CAN UNDERSTAND YOU
AND KNOW HOW TO BEST HELP YOU.

THE TROUBLE IS,
BY THE TIME YOU'VE UNLOADED IT ALL,
YOUR TIME IS UP
AND YOU'RE BOOKING YOUR NEXT APPOINTMENT.

I TOLD MY THERAPIST
ON THE SECOND APPOINTMENT,
"LAST WEEK WAS HARD BRINGING EVERYTHING UP
AND, TO BE HONEST, I CAME OFF THE PHONE
IN A WORSE STATE THAN BEFORE WE SPOKE AND
I CAN'T HAVE ANOTHER WEEK LIKE LAST WEEK!"

IT WASN'T AS BAD AS THE PREVIOUS WEEK
AND IT GRADUALLY GOT EASIER AND EASIER.

<u>IT'S WORTH TAKING THOSE NERVOUS STEPS
TOWARDS GETTING COUNSELLING
FOR THE BENEFITS YOU MAY REAP.</u>

STICK WITH IT FOR A FEW SESSIONS
AND IF IT'S REALLY NOT HELPING,
TRY SPEAKING WITH
A DIFFERENT COUNSELLOR,
AS EVERY ONE HAS THEIR OWN STYLE
AND APPROACH (AND ABILITY).

O.
DON'T SUFFER IN SILENCE.

<u>IF THINGS ARE REALLY BAD
AND YOU FEEL SUICIDAL
PLEASE **DIAL 111** (UK),
CALL **THE SAMARITANS**,
CALL **EMERGENCY SERVICES**,
CALL **YOUR GP**, OR
GOOGLE WHERE YOU CAN GET HELP, ETC...</u>

DON'T BE SHY...THESE PEOPLE CHOSE THESE JOBS
BECAUSE THEY WANT TO HELP PEOPLE.

<u>NOTHING IN THIS WORLD IS WORTHY
OF MAKING YOU FEEL THAT BAD</u>,
SO IF YOU *DO* FEEL THAT BAD,
TREAT YOURSELF TO SOME CARE.

REMEMBER, <u>THERE IS ALWAYS SOMEONE,
WHETHER IN FLESH OR IN SPIRIT,
WHO WOULD BE ABSOLUTELY CRUSHED
IF ANYTHING BAD HAPPENED TO YOU.</u>

YOU ARE LOVED. *LOVE YOURSELF.*

P.
**TRY TO LIVE HOW YOU WANT THEM
TO SEE YOU LIVING.**

THEY STILL WANT THE BEST FOR US.
THEY ARE URGING US NOT TO BE TOO SAD.
<u>THEY WANT TO SEE US LIVING LIFE HAPPILY.</u>
WHEN WE CRY, THEY CRY.
<u>WHEN WE SMILE, THEY SMILE.</u>
WHEN WE SUCCEED, THEY CHEER!

Q.
**REMEMBER...YOU WILL SEE
AND HOLD THEM AGAIN, I PROMISE.**

I KNOW THIS TO BE TRUE, BECAUSE I HAVE
SEEN AND HELD MY QUEEN IN MY ARMS

IN DREAM-VISIONS, WHERE I COULD
ACTUALLY FEEL HER IN MY ARMS!

IN ONE VISION, I ACTUALLY WONDERED IF I WAS
DREAMING, BUT, HAVING TAKEN SOME BREATHS
I CONCLUDED IT WAS REAL!

<u>UNTIL YOU SEE THEM AGAIN,
REMEMBER YOU ARE STILL HERE FOR A REASON.</u>

BE THE MOST POSITIVE YOU...
...THAT'S ALL YOU HAVE TO DO
TO FULFILL YOUR MISSION HERE!

R.
GRIEVE *YOUR* WAY.

DO WHATEVER YOU FEEL THE NEED TO DO
IN ORDER TO COPE WITH AND PROCESS
THE SHOCKING EVENTS YOU HAVE EXPERIENCED.

<u>NO ONE CAN TELL YOU WHAT IS
THE RIGHT OR WRONG WAY TO GRIEVE,</u>
FOR "WHO FEELS IT, KNOWS IT".
<u>AS LONG AS IT BRINGS NO HARM TO YOU
OR OTHERS, JUST DO WHATEVER YOU CAN TO COPE.</u>
KEEP THE PLACE THE SAME
OR TOTALLY RE-DECORATE,
IT'S UP TO YOU.

GET AWAY FOR A FEW DAYS IF YOU CAN.
STAY BY A FRIEND OR RELATIVE.

GO TO THE BEACH. GO TO THE COUNTRYSIDE.
GET A DOG. THEY ARE GREAT FOR COMPANY
AND THEY GET YOU OUT THE HOUSE FOR WALKS.
THEY ALSO HAVE A CALMING EFFECT ON US;
WHEN A DOG ENTERS THE ROOM
OUR BLOOD PRESSURE LOWERS!
JUST GO BY FEEL
AND TRY TO KEEP YOUR MIND IN THE MOMENT,
RATHER THAN IN THE PAST OR
WORRYING ABOUT THE FUTURE.

S.
TRY NOT TO OVER-THINK

THERE MAY BE A LOT GOING ON, OR TO DO,
LIKE ORGANISING THE FUNERAL
OR LETTING PEOPLE KNOW WHAT HAS HAPPENED,
BUT DON'T THINK ABOUT IT ALL AT ONCE,
THAT COULD BE OVERWHELMING.

<u>JUST FOCUS ON ONE THING AT A TIME.</u>
YOU WILL GET EVERYTHING SORTED, DON'T WORRY.
AND IF ANYTHING DOES GO WRONG...
...YOU KNOW THEY WILL BE LAUGHING IN SPIRIT,
FOR <u>SENSE OF HUMOUR DOES NOT DIE,</u>
<u>NOR DOES ANYTHING GOOD</u>
<u>ABOUT THEIR PERSONALITY CEASE TO EXIST.</u>

THEY ARE STILL THEMSELVES.
THEY ARE ALIVE AND WELL.
THEY ARE SAFE.
ALL IS WELL
AND ALL WILL BE WELL.

**T.
REMEMBER THAT
EVERYTHING HAPPENS FOR A REASON.**

MY WIFE ALWAYS USED TO SAY,
"EVERYTHING HAPPENS
THE WAY GOD WANTED IT TO HAPPEN!"
THAT'S COMING FROM SOMEONE
WHO GREW UP IN APARTHEID AND
HAD A VERY STRICT AND PAINFUL LIFE AND
WOULD BE FORGIVEN IF SHE WAS ANGRY AT GOD.
BUT SHE WAS SO PHILOSOPHICAL ABOUT THINGS.

<u>WHETHER WE LIVE A HUNDRED YEARS,
OR A THOUSAND YEARS,
IT'S NEVER LONG ENOUGH,
SO ENJOY IT, *ALL OF IT*, THE GOOD *AND* THE BAD,
OR SPEND ETERNITY IN SPIRIT WISHING YOU DID!</u>

**U.
GO TO SEE A PSYCHIC MEDIUM
OR VISIT A SPIRITUALIST CHURCH.**

A GENUINE PSYCHIC WILL GIVE YOU
PERSONAL INFORMATION THAT WILL
HELP YOU BELIEVE/UNDERSTAND THE IDEA
THAT <u>YOUR LOVED ONES AREN'T REALLY DEAD,
ONLY THEIR BODIES ARE.</u>
I WAS SKEPTICAL WHEN I WENT,
THINKING THEY MIGHT JUST BE MIND-READING.
SO WHEN I WAS BEING GIVEN A READING,

I JUST SAID MY WIFE'S NAME
OVER AND OVER IN MY HEAD
TO SEE IF THAT'S WHAT THEY WOULD SAY.

"THERE'S A BEAUTIFUL DARK GIRL HERE!",
THE LADY BEGAN!

"OH WHAT A BEAUTIFUL SMILE SHE'S GOT!",
SHE CONTINUED.
"IS IT YOUR GIRLFRIEND OR PARTNER?",
SHE ASKED.

"YES, IT'S MY WIFE.", I CONFIRMED.

"DID SHE LIKE WEARING BEADS ACROSS HER FORHEAD?

"AND DID SHE LIKE COOKING
LOTS OF LITTLE DISHES AT THE SAME TIME
AND YOU TAKE A BIT OF EACH?"

<u>I WAS AMAZED AT SUCH DETAILED FACTS.</u>
SHE SAID EVERYTHING *BUT* HER NAME!
THEN ANOTHER LADY ASKED ME
IF THERE WAS ANYONE I KNEW IN SPIRIT,
WHO LIKED MOTORBIKES.

THAT WAS MY DAD!
HE USED TO RIDE A BSA MOTORBIKE
ON "THE WALL OF DEATH"
AT THE KURSAAL, IN SOUTHEND, IN THE 60'S.
"RICKY, THE YOUNGEST
WALL OF DEATH RIDER IN THE WORLD!"

<u>IT IS REAL AND YOU CAN EVEN
LEARN TO DO IT YOURSELF!</u>
MEDIUMSHIP THAT IS,
NOT WALL OF DEATH RIDING!

[P.S. <u>DON'T BE TEMPTED TO DO OUIJA BOARDS!</u>
TOO MUCH NEGATIVITIY CAN COME
FROM USING THEM!]

V.
LOOK OUT FOR SIGNS.

<u>IF YOU KEEP AN OPEN MIND
YOU WILL BE SHOWN SOME KIND OF SIGN/S,</u>
BUT YOU HAVE TO REACH
A CERTAIN LEVEL OF STILLNESS FIRST,
OTHERWISE YOUR GRIEF CAN BLOCK THE SIGNS.
THEY CAN BE ANYTHING FROM
RECURRING NUMBERS, OR NUMBER PLATES,
TO WHITE FEATHERS, ROBINS OR EVEN THEIR SCENT.
A SPECIAL TUNE MAY PLAY ON THE RADIO
THAT NEVER USUALLY GETS PLAYED.

BEFORE THE INQUEST FINALLY BEGAN,
I HAD TO GO TO LONDON TO MEET MY LEGAL TEAM.
I WAS FULL OF NERVES AS I APPROACHED THE TRAIN.
I WALKED DOWN THE PLATFORM A BIT,
THEN CHOSE A DOOR, GOT ON BOARD
AND DUCKED INTO MY SEAT.
AS I SAT THERE, I LOOKED DOWN AT THE FLOOR,
THERE WAS A WHITE FEATHER BY MY FEET!
JUST LIKE ON THE FIRST DAY OF THE INQUEST.

INCIDENTLY, THE FIRST DAY OF THE INQUEST
WAS MONDAY THE 9TH OF AUGUST.
MY WIFE DIED ON MONDAY THE 9TH OF MAY.
MONDAY THE 9TH PRECEEDS FRIDAY THE 13TH.
MAY AND AUGUST ARE SIGNIFICANT,
AS ARE THE DATES.

KHABI'S BODY WAS LAID TO REST AUGUST THE 30TH.
SHE WAS BORN DECEMBER THE 30TH.
I WAS BORN JULY 30TH.
HER BROTHER, LEFA, HAD A BABY BOY, ON MAY 30TH.

"LIFE IS ONE BIG ROAD WITH LOTS OF SIGNS.
SIGN AND MORE SIGN!" - SUNG BY TENOR SAW.

CHECK OUT THE NUMBER PLATES
ON THESE CARS I SAW:

LOOK AT THIS ONE, **"KABI"**,
PARKED BEHIND THE CHURCH I VISITED
TO THANK THEM FOR THEIR SUPPORT AND KINDNESS.

AND THIS ONE...

...PARKED IN FRONT OF MUM'S CAR,
OUTSIDE MY FLAT;
"KKX" FOR KHABI AND KaRa X
LOOK AT THE MAKE'S BADGE....**"S"** FOR STUART.
LOOK AT THE HEART HANGING FROM THE MIRROR.
THE MESSAGE IS LOTS OF LOVE TO ME
FROM MY WIFE AND DAUGHTER!

I'M NOT SUGGESTING
THAT KHABI PUT THOSE CARS THERE,
OR THAT SHE CREATED THEIR NUMBER PLATES,
BUT <u>SHE KNEW THEY WERE THERE AND SHE DEFINITELY WANTED ME TO SEE THEM</u>,
HOPING I WOULD UNDERSTAND.
I DO, DARLING! X

W.
TRY I.A.D.C.
"INDUCED AFTER DEATH COMMUNICATION."

GO TO AFTERLIFECONNECTIONS.ORG.
THERE YOU WILL FIND LOTS OF INFO TO READ
BEFORE YOU REACH A LINK
TO A FREE GUIDED MEDITATION.

THIS MEDITATION MAY HELP YOU
TO HAVE AN EXPERIENCE WITH THE SPIRIT
OF YOUR LOVED ONE/S!

IT IS BASED ON A TECHNIQUE,
DISCOVERED BY ACCIDENT,
BY DR ALAN BOTKINS,
WHILST TREATING VIETNAM VETERANS
FOR POST TRAUMATIC STRESS DISORDER (PTSD),
USING EYE MOVEMENT DESENSITIZATION
AND REPROCESSING (EMDR).
DURING THIS TREATMENT,
A PATIENT CLOSED HIS EYES
AND HAD A VISION OF HIS DEAD COMRADES
WHO SALUTED HIM AND COMMENDED HIS ACTIONS.

IT WAS DISMISSED AS A HALLUCINATION
OR A TRICK OF THE MIND...
...BUT A NURSE WHO HAD BEEN TRAINED IN IADC
WAS GIVING THE TREATMENT TO HER PATIENT,
WHEN SHE, HERSELF, SAW A VISION OF A WOMAN
COMING TO VISIT HER PATIENT.

IT WAS THE PATIENTS' MOTHER.
SHE SAW HER WEARING THE SAME CLOTHES
HER PATIENT DESCRIBED HER WEARING IN HER VISION!
<u>THE FACT THAT A THIRD PARTY WITNESSED
THE SPIRITUAL VISITATION
PROVES IT WAS A REAL EVENT</u>
AND NOT SOME WISHFUL THINKING.
IT IS AN EMOTIONAL EXPERIENCE, SO ONLY DO IT
IF YOU ARE FEELING STRONG ENOUGH
TO COPE WITH THE EMOTIONS.
IT IS INCREDIBLE, THOUGH, I MUST SAY!

X.
CELEBRATE THEIR SOULDAY.

WE WERE ALIVE BEFORE OUR BODIES WERE.
<u>OUR BIRTHDAY WAS NOT THE BEGINNING OF OUR LIFE,
IT WAS JUST THE DAY WE CAME TO EARTH.
OUR "EARTHDAY".
THE DAY SOMEONE "DIES",
IS JUST THE DAY THEY WERE BORN (BACK) INTO SPIRIT.
IT'S THEIR "SOULDAY"!
IT IS A DAY TO BE CELEBRATED LIKE A BIRTHDAY,
BECAUSE IT'S A BIRTH INTO A NEW LIFE</u>...A NEW LIGHT!

RESTORED **I**N **P**ERFECTION,
THEY GO BACK TO THE HEIGHT OF HEALTH
AND LOOK THE WAY THEY DID IN THEIR YOUTH,
IF THEY WISH!
NO NEED TO REST IN PEACE
WHEN YOU HAVE NO MUSCLES TO TIRE;
NO WEIGHT TO BARE; NO NIGHT TO SLEEP THROUGH!

I KNOW YOU PROBABLY FEEL SICK
WHEN THE ANNIVERSARY COMES AROUND,
BUT <u>TRY TO REMEMBER</u>...
...THAT DAY WAS TERRIBLY SAD FOR US...
...BUT IT WAS THE BEGINNING
OF AN *AMAZING NEW LIFE* FOR THEM,
FILLED WITH WONDER,
VOID OF DANGER.

TRY TO BE HAPPY FOR THEM
AND, IN TIME, SMILE AGAIN!

Y.
REMEMBER THE SCIENCE.

ENERGY CANNOT BE CREATED
OR DESTROYED,
IT CAN ONLY CHANGE
FROM ONE STATE TO ANOTHER.
<u>THE BODY RETURNS TO THE ELEMENT IT IS MADE OF:
EARTH.</u>
<u>THE SPIRIT RETURNS TO THE ELEMENT IT IS MADE OF:
LIGHT.</u>

<u>THE BODY NOURISHES THE SOIL.</u>
<u>THE SOUL FLOURISHES IN THE LIGHT.</u>

<u>NOTHING CAN BE WIPED FROM EXISTANCE,
ONLY TRANSFORMED.</u>

TRY TO ERADICATE A SIMPLE PIECE OF PAPER.
IT CANNOT BE DONE:

TEAR IT UP...IT STILL EXISTS AS TINY PIECES.
BURN IT...AND IT WILL TURN TO SMOKE,
HEAT AND LIGHT.

IT MAY NOT BE PAPER ANYMORE...BUT IT STILL EXISTS
AS THE SMOKE IT GAVE OFF HAS CONTRIBUTED
TO THE ELEMENTS IN THE AIR, PERMANENTLY.
WHEN A BODY DIES...MIND AND SPIRIT REMAIN.

NO ONE EVER DIED...EXCEPT DEATH ITSELF, MAYBE.

Z.
RECOGNIZE TRANSIENCE.

EVERYTHING IS TEMPORARY.
NOTHING IS CONSTANT,
EXCEPT FOR CHANGE!

<u>THE PAIN YOU ARE FEELING
IS ONLY HOW YOU FEEL *NOW*.</u>

<u>IT WILL CHANGE IN TIME.
JUST DON'T GIVE UP.</u>

<u>GOOD THINGS ARE COMING Y/OUR WAY.</u>

EVERY TEAR WE SHED
IS A DOWN-PAYMENT ON A FUTURE GLORY.

<u>YOU *WILL* HEAL. YOU *WILL* SMILE. YOU *WILL* LOVE.</u>

IDENTIFY THE POSITIVE THINGS
THAT PLEASE YOUR SOUL;
THE THINGS YOU USED TO LOVE DOING;
THE PLACES YOU USED TO VISIT;
THE FOODS YOU USED TO EAT;
THE MUSIC YOU USED TO LISTEN TO;
THE THINGS YOU ENJOYED,
BUT HAVEN'T DONE FOR A LONG TIME.

RE-INTRODUCE THESE THINGS BACK INTO YOUR LIFE
AS MUCH AS POSSIBLE.

<u>YOU DESERVE TO BE HAPPY.
THE ONES WE MISS WANT US TO BE HAPPY.</u>

OPEN THE CURTAINS, LET THE LIGHT IN
AND EMBRACE THE FUTURE,
KNOWING THE ETERNAL, UNIVERSAL TRUTH:

THERE IS
NO END
TO LIFE
OR LOVE!

**EVEN IF IT DOESN'T SEEM LIKE IT,
ALL WILL BE WELL AND
ALL IS WELL.
<u>THEY SURVIVED.
SO MUST YOU.
AND SO YOU SHALL,
AS I HAVE!</u>**

BY KNOWING THE TRUTH,
RECOGNIZING THE SIGNS,
MEDITATING AND EXERCISING,
EATING AND RESTING WELL,
TREATING MYSELF FOR SHOCK AND
GETTING THERAPY, BUT, MOST IMPORTANTLY
WITH THE LOVE AND SUPPORT OF
FRIENDS AND FAMILY,
I STARTED TO PUT WEIGHT BACK ON
AND STARTED GOING OUT AND
BEGAN SOCIALISNG AGAIN…

"KEETY"   *CLIVEY*

...AND FOUND MYSELF
SMILING AGAIN.

NOW, I AM OPTIMISTIC OF THE FUTURE.
I FEEL SAFER THAN I DID.
I'M ABLE TO LIVE AT HOME AGAIN.
I'M ABLE TO LIVE, PERIOD.
AS WILL YOU!

<u>PLEASE DON'T GIVE UP!</u>

<u>ALL IS NOT WHAT IT SEEMS.</u>

<u>LOOK BEYOND THE SURFACE.</u>

<u>REMEMBER THE ETERNAL TRUTHS.</u>

<u>NOTHING IN THIS WORLD IS WORTHY
OF ROBBING YOU OF YOUR HAPPINESS.</u>

<u>FOR YOUR SAKE - AND
FOR THE SAKE OF THE SPIRITS AROUND YOU
AND FOR YOUR LIVING LOVED ONES,
FRIENDS AND FAMILY -
KEEP GOING!</u>

KEEP CALM. KEEP THE FAITH. KEEP WELL.
KEEP ON BEING YOU!
THAT'S WHAT WILL MAKE YOUR LOST LOVED ONES
AND YOUR LIVING LOVED ONES,
THE HAPPIEST.

WHEN KHABI WAS PREGNANT,
SHE WAS WORRIED ABOUT
THE STATE OF THE WORLD
AND KaRa'S SAFETY IN IT.

I PROMISED HER,
"DON'T WORRY BABE,
I'M GONNA MAKE THE CHANGES IN SOCIETY
THAT WILL MAKE THE WORLD SAFER FOR HER!"

I HAD NO IDEA HOW TO GO ABOUT DOING THAT...
...I JUST KNEW I *HAD* TO DO *SOMETHING!*

I HOPE THAT THE TRAGIC EVENTS
AS WELL AS THE AMAZING PHENOMENA
THAT HAVE TAKEN PLACE
AND HAVE BEEN RECORDED IN THIS BOOK
MAY, IRONICALLY, HELP TO KEEP THAT PROMISE.

IF I CAN ONLY CHANGE *YOUR* WORLD
BY EASING YOUR PAIN
BY GIVING YOU HOPE AND COMFORT,
KNOWLEDGE AND TRUTH,
WELL THAT'S EQUALLY WONDERFUL!

INNER PEACE AND HEALING TO YOU ALL.

ONE ETERNAL LOVE!

* * *

THANK YOU SO MUCH FOR TAKING THE TIME
TO READ MY BOOK!
IT'S BEEN EMOTIONAL FOR ME TO WRITE...
...AND FOR YOU TO READ, I'M SURE...BUT,
I REALLY HOPE IT HAS CHANGED YOUR LIFE
IN SOME POSITIVE WAY!

IT'S DONE *ME* GOOD.
I FEEL HEARD. I FEEL UNDERSTOOD
AND I FEEL LIGHTER.
IT WAS VERY HARD TO WRITE,
EMOTIONALLY AND TECHNICALLY
OFTEN MAKING ME CRY IN SADNESS
AND SHOUT IN FRUSTRATION,
BUT I DO FEEL BETTER NOW IT'S DONE
AND I'M HOPEFUL IT WILL HELP YOU HEAL.

SOME GOOD HAS TO COME
FROM THIS AWFUL EXPERIENCE.
I MUST ALCHEMIZE THE DROSS
TO BE LEFT WITH SOMETHING PRECIOUS.

I HAVE LEARNED THAT NOTHING IS RANDOM;
THAT THERE IS A DIVINE PATTERN AND PLAN
TO EVERY SINGLE EVENT.
EVERYTHING HAPPENS FOR A REASON
AND EVERYTHING HAS A SEASON.
DESPITE APPEARANCES,
ALL IS AS IT SHOULD BE,
SO TRY TO BE POSITIVE.
NONE OF THE BAD STUFF REALLY MATTERS
IN THE GRAND, ETERNAL SCHEME OF THINGS!

**WE ARE ETERNAL BEINGS.
WE ARE ALL INVISIBLY CONNECTED.
WHAT YOU DO TO OTHERS,
YOU'RE ACTUALLY DOING TO YOURSELF,
SO *WHEN YOU HURT OTHERS,
YOUR HURTING YOUR OWN SOUL*.
SIMILARLY, THE WAY YOU TREAT YOURSELF,
YOU DO TO OTHERS, SPIRITUALLY.
SO, TO TRULY CARE FOR THE ONES YOU LOVE,
IS TO CARE FOR YOURSELF.
LIFE'S PRECIOUS, SO
LIVE IT WITH A SMILE ON YOUR FACE**

AND LOVE IN YOUR HEART!

KHABI
WAS/IS LOVED
BY SO MANY PEOPLE!

I MEAN TRULY LOVED.
BY A WHOLE COMMUNITY
OF BROTHERS AND SISTERS
ALL OVER THE WORLD.

WHEN SOMEONE IS KILLED
IT IS NOT JUST THE VICTIM
THAT IS AFFECTED,
BUT HUNDREDS MORE
WHO WILL MISS THAT PERSON
AND FEEL THE PAIN
OF THEIR LOSS!

ENOUGH VIOLENCE.
ENOUGH OF BULLYING AND BACK-STABBING.
LIFE IS TOO PRECIOUS.

EACH ONE OF US IS LOVED.
SOMEONE, MAYBE MANY,
WOULD BE UTTERLY DESTROYED
BY THE IDEA OF ANY HARM COMING TO YOU...

...AND EQUALLY DESTROYED
BY THE IDEA OF YOU HARMING ANYONE...
...INCLUDING YOURSELF.

IT'S TIME FOR LOVE TO RULE OUR HEARTS!

LIKE I SAID, A *LOT* OF PEOPLE
HAD/HAVE A LOT OF LOVE
FOR KHABI.

NEIGHBOURS GOT TOGETHER
AND HAD A PLAQUE
(TWO ACTUALLY!)
PLACED ON A BENCH
OUTSIDE OUR FLATS.
STRANGERS CAME FROM FAR
TO ATTEND HER FUNERAL.

EVEN THE TREES WILL MISS HER HUGS!

I LOVE YOU DARLING.
MY WIFE
FROM LIFE TO LIFE.

I HOPE WHAT HAPPENED TO YOU
PUTS A STOP TO/PREVENTS
A LOT OF PAIN IN THE WORLD.

SOAR THE HEIGHTS OF HEAVEN
AND DIVE THE DEEPNESS OF SPIRIT.
KISS KaRa FOR ME, "MUMMY-NYANA"!
I KNOW YOU ARE BOTH WITH ME ALWAYS.
I KNOW YOU'RE A GREAT MUM AND
BEING A DAD FEELS GREAT! THANK YOU!
I LOVE YOU BOTH SO VERY MUCH.
$X \infty X$

AFTERWORD

LIKE I SAID AT THE VERY BEGINNING OF THIS BOOK;
WHAT HAPPENED TO MY FAMILY
WAS <u>PREVENTABLE</u>.

WE RAISED THE ALARM
ABOUT THE DANGER AND INTIMIDATION
WE FELT AS A RESULT OF THE ACTIONS OF
SERIOUSLY MENTALLY ILL *PEOPLE*
BEING HOUSED IN OUR HOME.

WE REQUESTED INTERVENTION,
BUT THIS NEVER SEEMED TO HAPPEN.
WE INFORMED THE COUNCIL THAT
WE WERE GETTING BLAMED
FOR D.I.Y. NOISES AND PLAYING LOUD MUSIC
ALL THROUGH THE NIGHT
AND WERE RECEIVING NOTES OF COMPLAINT...
...EVEN THOUGH IT WASN'T US.

WE WEREN'T BELIEVED. WHY?
THE COUNCIL BELIEVED OUR TORMENTORS
OVER US. WHY?

OUR CONCERNS AND REQUESTS
WERE SEEMINGLY IGNORED,
WHILE COMPLAINTS *ABOUT US*
WERE HOTLY RESPONDED TO
AND SOUND RECORDING EQUIPMENT
WAS GOING TO BE INSTALLED TO MONITOR US!

THIS, EVEN THOUGH SOMEONE HAD TO
CALL THE POLICE TO ATTEND TO THE DISTURBANCES
COMING FROM SOME OTHER FLAT;
AND EVEN THOUGH I HAD PERSONALLY TOLD
THE COUNCIL THE NOISE WASN'T COMING FROM US,
WHEN THEY TURNED UP AT *MY* DOOR TO INVESTIGATE,
FINDING ME QUIETLY TYPING MY FIRST BOOK;
AND *EVEN THOUGH THEY KNEW
THAT THE PEOPLE COMPLAINING ABOUT US
HAD MENTAL HEALTH ISSUES.*

WHY???

WHY WAS I NOT BEING HEARD,
WHILE MY ACCUSORS WERE…
…I FEAR ONE REASON MAY BE
BECAUSE THEY LOOKED AT ME
AND DIDN'T BELIEVE I WASN'T GUILTY
OF ALL THE COMPLAINTS LEVELLED AT ME,
BASED ON HOW I LOOK.

IN OTHER WORDS:
PREJUDICE/RACISM/STEREO-TYPING.

SADLY,
THIS KIND OF TREATMENT
IS NOTHING NEW TO ME
AND OTHER PEOPLE OF COLOUR.
HENCE THE NEED TO ESTABLISH
IN THE MIND OF SOCIETY, THAT
<u>BLACK LIVES MATTER.</u>

YES, OF COURSE, *ALL LIVES* MATTER,
BUT *IT IS ONLY BLACK LIVES* THAT APPEAR
NOT TO MATTER....TO POLICE, COUNCILS,
GOVERNMENTS, COMMUNITIES, ETC...

LILLO WAS WANTED BY POLICE
FOR A DIFFERENT INCIDENT
AT THE TIME HE SET THE FIRE...
...BUT THE POLICE WERE APPARENTLY UNABLE
TO APPREHEND HIM DURING THE MONTHS
BETWEEN THEN AND THE FIRE.
WOULD THIS'VE BEEN THE CASE
IF HE'D 'AVE LOOKED LIKE ME???

WHITE KILLERS WALK FREELY, WHILST
A DISPROPORTIONATE NUMBER AND PERCENTAGE OF
BLACK MALE YOUNGSTERS ARE IMPRISONED
FOR MISDEMEANOURS.

THE WORLD MUST CHANGE
ON SO MANY LEVELS.
LOVE AND UNITY MUST BECOME HUMANITY'S GOAL.
<u>IT'S TIME TO REVIVE TRUE CARE.</u>

THE CHANGE STARTS WITH YOU AND ME.
LET US ALL LIVE IN LOVE, FOR,
"UNTIL THE PHILOSOPHY
WHICH HOLDS ONE RACE SUPERIOR
AND ANOTHER INFERIOR,
IS FINALLY AND PERMANENTLY
DISCREDITED AND ABANDONED...

"UNTIL THE COLOUR OF A MAN'S SKIN
IS OF NO MORE SIGNIFICANCE
THAN THE COLOUR OF HIS EYES...

"*UNTIL THAT DAY*, THE DREAM OF *LASTING PEACE,
WORLD CITIZENSHIP*
AND THE RULE OF *INTERNATIONAL MORALITY*
WILL REMAIN IN BUT A FLEETING ILLUSION,
TO BE *PERSUED*...
...BUT *NEVER* ATTAINED...

"BUT....*WE ARE CONFIDENT
IN THE VICTORY*...
...OF GOOD OVER EVIL."

– EMPEROR HAILE SELASSIE I,
SPEAKING TO THE LEAGUE OF NATIONS, 1966.

GOD IS LOVE:
WHAT IS NOT LOVING...
...IS NOT GODLY.

"LOVE THY NEIGHBOUR AS THYSELF"
"LOVE ONE ANOTHER, AS I HAVE LOVED YOU."
PROBABLY THE MOST IMPORTANT COMMANDMENTS
IN THE HOLY BIBLE.

ISLAM SOMETIMES CALLS GOD, "AL WADUD",
"THE MOST LOVING", IN ARABIC.
RASTAFARI SAY "WADADA",
"LOVE", IN AMHARIC.

LOVE IS THE ONLY WAY FORWARD.

I WOULD IMAGINE,
VERY FEW OF US ARE HAPPY
WITH THE WAY THE WORLD IS,
SO RATHER THAN JUST PUTTING UP WITH IT,
OR PERPETUATING THE NEGATIVITY,
LET US STAND FOR CHANGE:
A CHANGE IN MIND-SET,
A CHANGE IN HEART.

TRUTH WILL EASE THE PAIN
IN OUR HEARTS
AND
LOVE WILL EASE THE PAIN
IN THE WORLD.

AS MY FATHER SO RIGHTLY SAID TO ME:

**"LOVE IS THE ONLY THING
WE NEED TO BE GROWING
AMONG THE PEOPLE
IN ORDER FOR THIS UNIVERSE
TO FIND THE BALANCE
WHICH IT LOST SOMEHOW,
SOMEWHERE."**

LOVE *IS* RISING!

NOTES:

Some "coincidences"/patterns/<u>signs</u>:

30th July, Stuart was born.
30th December, Khabi was born.
30th August, Khabi's body buried.
30th May, Khabi's nephew was born.
30 years young Khabi "died".

9th May, Khabi and Stuart met.
9th May, Khabi "died". Friday 13th followed.
9th May Lillo arrested for threats, but released.
9th August, Inquest. Friday 13th followed.
9 years between (step) Dad & Khabi R.I.P.

Richard was Stuart's (step) Dad's name.
Richard was Khabi's landlord's name.
Richard was the one who tried to save Khabi.
Richard drove Stu to collect Khabi's parents.

8 years they were together.
8 months pregnant when she "died".
8th Floor the killer lived on.
8th of May, KaRa "died".

NOTES:

11th May, Khabi and Stu married.
11th May, Lillo re-arrested for the fire.
11 was the total of Lillo's age at the time.
11 was the total of Lillo's door number.
11:11 pm was the time of first call to 999.

Stu's "step" Dad left his life, physically @ 63.
Stu's biological Dad came into his life @ 63.
6+3=9. Two more "9" signs to add to the list.

*(from p.55) Carly eventually got sick
and was struggling to walk or even stand.
My mum and I took her to the vet,
hoping they could help her.
It poured with torrential rain on the way.
I knew what this meant. Tears from Heaven.
[It rained 1 months worth in 1 day
when Khabi "died".] They told us there was nothing
they could do for her. We were absolutely devastated.
We couldn't just give up on her after everything
she'd done for us. But we had to admit, it really was
the most humane thing to do for her...and...

NOTES:

...it is very different
from Khabi's passing,
worse in some sense, because this time,
I actually WAS responsible for the death.
I felt like I'd let her down....betrayed her, even.
It was awful...but I know
there was no other option...and besides...
...she is back with her best friend, Khabi, now!

ALL IS WELL X

Carly was put to sleep – 7/4/22,
exactly one month before the
6th anniversary of the fire – 7/5/22.
12 years old, she was.

The next morning, I heard her claws
tapping on the hard floor, outside my door!
Same thing next day, too!
Mum also heard her during the night!
She's OK, bless her. X

NOTES:

"<u>GUILTINESS, REST(S) ON THEIR CONSCIENCE,</u>
OH YEAH!....AND THEY LIVE A LIFE
OF FALSE PRETENCE, EVERYDAY....
"THESE ARE THE BIG FISH, WHO ALWAYS TRY
TO EAT DOWN THE SMALL FISH....
"THEY WOULD DO ANYTHING
TO MATERIALIZE THEIR EVERY WISH!....
"BUT WAIT! <u>WOE TO THE DOWN-PRESSORS!
THEY'LL EAT THE BREAD OF SORROW!</u>
"WOE TO THE DOWN-PRESSORS!
THEY'LL EAT THE BREAD OF SAD TOMORROW!"
- FROM BOB MARLEY'S, "GUILTINESS".

"WHY DO YOU LOOK SO SAD AND FORSAKEN?
DON'T YOU KNOW, WHEN ONE DOOR IS CLOSED
ANOTHER IS OPEN!?!
<u>WOULD YOU LET THE SYSTEM
MAKE YOU KILL YOUR BROTHER MAN?
NO, DREAD, NO!
WOULD YOU LET THE SYSTEM GET ON TOP
YOUR HEAD? AGAIN, NO, DREAD, NO</u>!
"...THE BIGGEST MAN YOU EVER DID SEE
WAS ONCE A BABY!"
- FROM BOB MARLEY'S,
"COMING IN FROM THE COLD".

NOTES:

IF YOU KNOW SOMEONE
WHO HAS LOST SOMEONE
IN A VIOLENT/SHOCKING WAY,
PLEASE BE GENTLE WITH THEM,
EVEN IF IT WAS MANY YEARS AGO,
FOR OUR HEARTS CAN BE
SO VERY TENDER STILL,
EVEN THOUGH IT MAY NOT SHOW.

<u>BE KIND TO ONE ANOTHER.</u>
<u>BE KIND TO YOURSELVES.</u>

ENJOY BEING A LOVING, CARING PERSON!

BE GOOD...
...AND MAY ONLY GOOD AND PLEASANT THINGS
COME YOUR WAY, ALWAYS!

Stu Abrey
X

NOTES:

THIS ADVICE
MAY SAVE A LIFE:

AS MY DAD ONCE SAID;

"IF EVER YOU'RE IN DANGER...
...DON'T SHOUT, "HELP"...
...SHOUT, "FIRE!""

PEOPLE WILL BE TOO AFFRAID
TO COME FOR HELP,
BUT
SAY THERE'S A FIRE
AND EVERYONE WANTS TO SEE!